ADVANCE PRAISE FOR J.M. KEARNS'
Why Mr. Right Can't Find You

"...the smartest piece on the male–female disconnect I have read all year. I wanted to send it to all my single girlfriends—and even some of my married ones."
~ Sheree-Lee Olson, Style Editor at *The Globe and Mail*

"Kearns...offers what I consider a literary MRI of the male brain."
~ Georgie Binks, CBC News Viewpoint

"J.M. Kearns' *Why Mr. Right Can't Find You* really gets at the roots of attraction between men and women in an intelligent, useful way. It will give women some radically honest insights into how men look for love, and it will empower them to play a more active, adventurous role in finding Mr. Right. He's out there, for sure— and this is the only map you need."
~ Marni Jackson, award-winning author and journalist

"J.M. Kearns' "How Men Choose Women" [Chapter 3 of this book] may well be the most insightful 11 pages I've encountered on that subject."
~ Wendy McElroy, *The Globe and Mail*

"J.M. Kearns deftly explains what men are looking for when seeking a woman to date."
~ Colin Hunter, *The Kitchener-Waterloo Record*

"...a real contribution to better understanding between the sexes. J.M. Kearns gives the lowdown on what a man is really thinking as he sizes up a woman (it's better than you think)."
~ Nicole Langlois, *The London Free Press*

Ordinary readers who read early releases of the book were deeply affected by it. Here is what they had to say:

"This book...makes you look at relationships from a completely different perspective. I approached someone through an avenue I had never thought of before (because Kearns helped me to see opportunities, and empowered me to do something about it) and we have been dating ever since. The difference about this relationship is that I didn't approach it with a sense of lack or deficiency. This is truly a new day and a new way for me!"

~ Lorraine L.

"*Why Mr. Right Can't Find You* is the book of hope. I saw a great new man, followed the advice in this book, and now I'm happily married to him!"

~ Olivia D.

"What J.M. Kearns had to say about compatibility rang true: it gave voice to a part of my own personal knowledge. It helped me make an important change and find a better relationship."

~ Jeannie L.

"This book does even more than it thinks it's doing—it's good for *men*, too! After reading it I became very aware that you can't just let 'sightings' pass you by. You have to be willing to take chances. J.M. Kearns helped me remember that men and women are on the same side—that someone was out there looking for me, and *wanted* me to find her. Since reading it, an amazing opportunity came my way, and I didn't blow it. Now we are dating seriously."

~ Gordon Vincent

If you have an experience or insight to share as a result of reading this book, please visit www.WhyMrRight.com.

WHY MR. RIGHT CAN'T FIND YOU

The Surprising Answers that Will Change Your Life—and His

J.M. Kearns

John Wiley & Sons Canada, Ltd.

National Library of Canada Cataloguing in Publication Data

Kearns, J. M. (J. Michael)
Why Mr. Right can't find you / J.M. Kearns.

ISBN: 978-0-470-83956-0

1. Mate selection. 2. Man-woman relationships. I. Title.

HQ801.K42 2007   646.7'8   C2006-905934-9

Production Credits
Cover design: Ian Koo
Cover illustrations: © iStockphoto.com/Jennifer Borton
Interior text design: Adrian So R.G.D
Interior layout: Tegan Wallace
Author photo: Debra Donahue
Wiley Bicentennial Logo: Richard J. Pacifico
Printer: Friesens

This book is printed with biodegradable vegetable-based inks on 55lb Hi-Bulk Cream paper with 100% post-consumer waste.

John Wiley & Sons Canada, Ltd.
6045 Freemont Blvd.
Mississauga, Ontario
L5R 4J3

Printed in Canada

1 2 3 4 5 FP 11 10 09 08 07

TABLE OF CONTENTS

PREFACE

$\mathcal{I}$ never intended to become an expert on Why Mr. Right Can't Find You. I would rather have found the right woman and had a long, hearty marriage, like my parents. But it didn't work out that way, and the years of searching taught me a lot.

I fell in love, I had relationships, but they didn't last. I got over thinking it was the other person's fault; I even got past thinking it was mine, because I eventually saw that two people have to be compatible. For years I searched for the right person: I knew so much about her, could imagine her, but I couldn't find her. A lot of my male friends were the same. We had grown up, we had the best of intentions, we wanted a lifetime partner.

I also knew some married couples very well, and heard from many more when I was a crisis counsellor. And mostly they weren't happy. I wondered if it was better to be alone. Then it occurred to me that people can't choose the right person *if they don't have enough of a choice.*

I saw that single men are constantly looking, but the women they *really* want to meet are not in sight. This seemed a waste of valuable male yearning—including mine! I thought, *This can be changed*. Being a practical philosopher, I began to develop a theory about how the woman of my dreams could help me find her. I came upon some excellent methods women could use to connect with the good men who are looking for them. I started writing this book. I guess in the back of my mind a voice said, *Some day my Ms. Right will read these words and they'll do the trick.*

While researching the book, I interviewed many single women, in person and online. I ran my ideas past them, and their response surprised me. They resisted the very approaches that I thought would solve the problem. They didn't want to be proactive about finding a mate. I asked them why, and they gave me some interesting answers. To me it seemed that various beliefs and myths were holding them back, and keeping them from being optimistic. I saw that my book would have to combat those myths, and I started writing those chapters.

Then one night at 2 a.m. I got an Instant Message. A woman had found my profile on AOL, where I had described myself and the woman of my dreams. She had gone searching for the man she wanted. She searched on two words and they led her to me. Sparks flew, we exchanged photos (lots of them), and we talked on the phone, many long conversations. But there was a hitch. She lived a thousand miles away. We decided to meet in person and after that we couldn't turn back. Within six months we loaded up a U-Haul truck and brought our lives together. Today we're still going strong, and I am grateful every day that she overcame the myths and fears and reached out to where I could reach her.

The completion of my manuscript was inspired by what she did: She showed me that my ideas were on the right track. This book goes out on behalf of all the men who sincerely want to find a lifetime partner, to all the women who want the same thing.

INTRODUCTION

*J*oday a man is looking for you.

Out there in the world, he is searching; even when he's occupied with other things, you're in the back of his mind. Other areas of his life are looking good. He works hard and is moving towards his goals. He has a social life, has good friends of both genders, but it isn't enough. He is unattached. He can handle life that way, but he isn't satisfied. He hasn't found the woman of his dreams.

That's because he hasn't found *you*. For you are it: You are the one he wants and needs, the one he imagines.

And guess what? The reverse is also true. He is your Mr. Right. He is the one you want, the one you are imagining.

I'm not saying you spend your time pining for a man you haven't met. Like him, you make it just fine on your own. (In fact, you probably do better on your own than most men.) But still, but still...you would rather have a partner sharing your life. And you don't want just anyone; you would rather have no one at all than settle for the wrong guy.

But what I am saying in this book is that *you don't have to settle*. You can have the right guy. He's out there looking for you now. If we could just get the two of you together in a room, talking to each other, nature would take its course. (Contrary to the dating books, if you get into a conversation with the right man you won't have a problem knowing what to say!)

Maybe this sounds too hopeful to you. Maybe you are in a bad relationship right now (perhaps a marriage, perhaps not), but it's going nowhere and you aren't happy in it. Or maybe you are alone: You got out of a bad relationship and you are trying to avoid a repeat. Either way, you may be discouraged about the chances of ever finding happiness with a mate. If you've read much in this area, you may even think it's something about you...

Many self-help books begin with the thinly veiled assumption that if you are single, you must be a loser, and that is *why* you are single. They say there is something defective about you and they are going to tell you how to "fix" yourself.

The world is full of lonely winners. I don't believe this. It isn't what I've seen out here in the real world where most of us live. What I have seen is that *the world is full of lonely winners.* There are a lot of really great men out there searching for someone and having no luck, and there are a lot of really great women also looking who are just what those men are searching for. But they aren't meeting each other. *That* is the problem.

Looking at the situation another way, let me ask you something:

Why do you think most relationships fail these days?

- Because people don't work at them?
- Because people are too busy in today's frantic world?
- Because the traditional values of fidelity and loyalty are dead?

I don't think so. The reason most relationships fail is simply this: *People are with the wrong people*. They pick the wrong partner and then waste years trying to make it work.

They choose wrongly, and then blame themselves when it turns out to be a detour into alienation.

And why do otherwise rational adult women and men choose the wrong partners?

Because *they don't have enough of a choice*.

And that happens because they don't *give* themselves enough of a choice.

THE CASTAWAY THEORY OF LOVE

There is a kind of castaway mentality that many people bring to the challenge of finding that special person.

The thinking goes something like, "I'll sit on this beach and see what the ocean tosses up on my shore—maybe something good will come along, like a rowboat or a crate of oranges or a lifetime partner."

We tend to think, if I'm meant to be with a certain person, life will do the work. Life will wash them up on my shore. So I will limit my romantic choices to the people whom I happen to meet.

Now that approach might work in high school and college, when new faces come at you all the time. And some people do get lucky at a young age and find a terrific mate. But after that it gets a lot harder. You meet a few unattached people at work, you meet a few through friends, but what are the odds? The cold fact is that if you limit your selection to the people whom life throws your way, you are likely to have a bad choice or none at all.

Many of us put more thought into finding a placemat than finding a mate.

What's needed is to treat the finding of a mate as a real, serious challenge, deserving of a real, serious effort. Many of us put more thought into finding a placemat than finding a mate. But it doesn't have to be that way.

Think for a moment of the effort you would put into finding a new job. You would polish your resumé, research employers in your area of choice, canvass Help Wanted ads in newspapers and online, buy fabulous new outfits, attend job fairs, send out letters of inquiry, make follow up calls, attend interviews... and the list goes on. You wouldn't just sit at home, hoping the right employer would knock on your door and humbly request your services. No—because such a major goal is worthy of a serious, sustained effort.

Now ask yourself, is finding a good mate any less important than finding a good job? Of course not. Yet many people wait passively for the right person to come along.

But why *should* you limit your selection? Why should you be passive?

Life is like a road trip: The best way to get where you're goin' is to climb out of the passenger seat and get behind the wheel.

You need to take charge of your own mating quest. You need to be proactive.

And the good news is, you are not alone in your quest. You have an ally, the best ally imaginable. You have Mr. Right looking for you.

I said this at the start, but it's time to look at the (very positive) implications. If you really entertain the thought that your Mr. Right is out there, it gives you a total change in perspective—a change to optimism. Imagine for a moment an unattached man out there searching, who is right for you, a good match for you in every important way.

That tells you several things.

It's you he is looking for—or he wouldn't *be* your Mr. Right.

He already likes your mind and your body and your smile and your style... or he wouldn't be your Mr. Right.

He is already someone you can love—for the same reason. So...

WHY HASN'T MR. RIGHT FOUND YOU YET?

Mr. Right is looking for you, but he hasn't found you—yet. When we look at the reasons why, we will see what you need to do to close the gap between you and him.

Men have gotten a lot of bad press in the relationship books. They are variously portrayed as aliens from Mars, speaking a separate language, mostly just looking for sex. In this book I will "rip the lid off the male psyche" to reveal... a different picture. I'll throw a fresh light on the errant but lovable souls of men, disclosing that there are lots of them out there who are looking for a meaningful relationship with a good woman. And I'll explore the actual ways—some of them loony and lazy—that real men search for, perceive, and choose the women they want to try for. What is a man thinking about when he looks at women? The answers may surprise you—in a good way.

Once we see how your intrepid dream lover conducts himself, we will be able to see why he hasn't found you yet. It will boil down to two problems.

The first is that he can't do it alone. His way of searching isn't perfect, it won't get him all the way to you.

The second problem is really the solution to the first. He needs your help. And strange as it may seem, so far he isn't getting it—or enough of it.

There are two main things you can do to help Mr. Right find you. The first is, *be more aware of opportunities that are already there.* One of my themes is that men and women who would be really good together are constantly passing each other by. Less like ships in the night than like preoccupied professionals in the day. In chapters like "Before You Can Mate, You Have to Meet: the underrated chance encounter" I will explore the surprising potential of these situations.

The second thing you can do is, *create new opportunities* for you and Mr. Right to find each other. This topic is a big one and occupies a lot of this book.

Let's start with him finding you. That's the old-fashioned way, the man as initiator, and it's a valid part of the story. You can help Mr. Right find you, by *making yourself more easily findable.* This may sound ludicrously simple, but if you want someone to find you, you need to *be where he is looking.* The fish idling in the rippled creek won't be caught by the fisherman out on the open lake. Better to put yourself where he searches, make yourself visible and approachable, and be alert to his possible presence. I will discuss practical ways, in the real world and online, that you can put yourself on the radar screen of the good man who is looking for you.

Last but not least, you can be the initiator. There's a new opportunity worthy of the name. Become the hunter, *go out and search for him*. On the proactive scale, that's the top of the line. And these days, it's very doable. We live in a wondrous age. The resources are there, online and off; you just have to be willing to use them. I'll discuss exactly how.

So, you can make yourself more findable, or go out on your own quest to find him. Or you can do both. You won't be surprised that my advice is, do both—and thereby double your chances.

Let's stop and take a little breath here. Faced with this idea, what are you feeling? What I have seen more than once when I've talked to women about making these changes is that they come up with reasons why this sort of plan won't work. Many women tend to resist this approach, and even to sabotage these possibilities when they arise by accident. They don't want to take charge of their own mating quest. They think it is against nature, or gender, or romance. Or destiny. They think it's embarrassing. They think Mr. Right won't recognize them—he has bad taste or he cares about the wrong things. (But then he wouldn't be Mr. Right, right?) They think the whole method won't work—or they're afraid it will work, and that isn't the way they want to meet their knight on the white charger.

And that's just the tip of the iceberg! Lots of mistaken or oversimplified beliefs get in the way of you and Mr. Right finding each other. To list just a few:

- The one and only man who is right for you was chosen by Destiny;
- You won't meet Mr. Right if you aren't dressed for the occasion;

- Men only care about looks, but true beauty is on the inside;
- All men are looking for the same kind of perfection, the one put forward by the media;
- A bar is not a place where you could meet a good man;
- Beware a man with baggage;
- If you have trust issues, carry a sign saying you're looking for Honesty;
- Opposites attract and make the best mates;
- A woman who conducts her own search for a good man, reveals herself to be "desperate for love."

The overarching myth, the one that provides a home for all the others, is that *true love only happens to the woman who doesn't seek it out. If she will just wait, the perfect man will ride into her life. (Or if he doesn't, she never could have found true love anyway.)*

Part One of this book concerns you and Mr. Right connecting in real world settings. It's called "Finding Mr. Right in the Real World." This section shoots down the myths, attitudes, and beliefs that discourage you from embracing the ultimate adventure. It gives you practical tips and advice on how to create and handle opportunities, covering topics like the underrated chance encounter, how women choose men, how men choose women, the best places to meet, and how to take advantage of them.

Once you put these approaches into practice, you will get results: namely, a series of encounters with promising candidates. How do you tell whether a given man is really right for you? If I am correct about why most relationships fail—

because people choose the wrong partners—then this question could not be more important. In answering it, we'll have to deal with a lot of phony wisdom that is floating around, and separate the real horse sense from the doggy doo. I'm talking about things like baggage, is it good or bad? Sexual attraction, should you trust it or not? Trust itself, how honest should a potential mate be, or claim to be? Wish lists, what do they prove? "Hopeless romantics," are they meant for each other? The things you have in common, which ones matter, which ones lie under the surface, how can you read them and weigh them rightly? How does he watch TV? How does he feel about masculinity? How do you? What can you read in his sense of humour?

What you need is an early warning system that can save you from unnecessary heartache and alert you to good news on the road ahead. So in Part Two, "Recognizing Mr. Right," I explore the false signs and the true signs of "rightness," the surprising keys to real compatibility, and the best ways to use them. Included in this section are topics like: The Six Factors in Sexual Compatibility (including a torrid exposé of the two types of kisser); body issues, and how to break free from the dubious norms of our culture; careers, jobs, money, and children; and values regarding politics and religion.

Part Three of this book is called "Finding Mr. Right Online." A woman who seriously wants to find a lifetime partner cannot afford to neglect the Internet. No resource in history has offered a chance to pick out exactly the people you are interested in from such a wide sample. There was a time when this method of meeting was still a work in progress, more likely to attract the adventurous or the weird; but that time has passed and the tipping point has been reached. There are now so many eligible men and women on the Internet that it is the place where you are most likely to find the person you are looking for—if you know how to use it. That is why I provide an in-depth, detailed guide to finding Mr. Right online. A lot of what I discuss in the first two parts of this book will matter in the third, for this simple reason:

The online journey is just a way of getting yourself to an in-person meeting with a desirable guy; and once that is achieved, the fact that you found him online matters much less than what goes on in person.

Not only that, but the ways people present themselves and perceive each other online turn out in many ways to mirror the real-world behavior I explore in Parts One and Two.

Among Part Three's topics will be

- Myth-busting 201: misconceptions about online dating;
- Dating sites: features you need;
- Look before you pay: the joys of free searching;
- A good photo set: what to shoot for;
- How to create a winning online ad;
- A portrait of three top sites;
- The curious case of eHarmony.com;
- Honesty and body image: how the Internet can set you free;
- How to eliminate Mr. Wrongs;
- What happens if you find Mr. Right and he isn't local? Are long-distance relationships worth bothering with?
- How to conduct an Internet romance; and why you should avoid falling in love before you meet in person;
- The first in-person meeting: what to wear, what to ask, what to watch for and watch out for.

I said a minute ago that this book is a guide to the ultimate adventure. And I meant it. Finding a mate can be a great and fun adventure, rather like a good day at Holt's. And when the search is over, then you will embark on the best adventure of all: living life with the right person.

1 PART
FINDING MR. RIGHT IN THE REAL WORLD

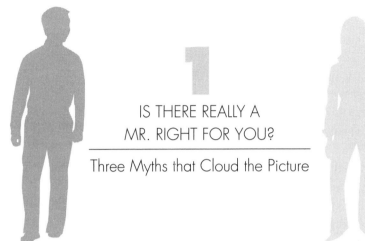

IS THERE REALLY A
MR. RIGHT FOR YOU?

Three Myths that Cloud the Picture

$\mathcal{T}$he short answer is yes. But first, what do women mean when they talk about their Mr. Right?

Mr. Right is a man with whom you could have a fulfilling long-term relationship. Fulfilling on all major levels, sexual and non-sexual. A guy you could be happy with. A guy who could become your soul mate, if given a chance, and who would value this enough to be honest and true to you.

When women talk about Mr. Right, they often assume a further point: *That there is only one of him.* Somewhere on the planet, the theory goes, there lurks "the one and only man who is meant for you!" If you can only bump into him, you can hardly go wrong! Sparks will fly and joy will be had! The problem is, what are the odds? Let's say there are roughly two billion adult males spread all over the planet, give or take a few million. Just one out of all these guys is the one you seek. One in two billion. This is not a cheerful picture.

And...maybe Mr. One and Only is married. Or he's single, but he lives in Bangkok, and is moving shortly to Somalia.

Even suppose he lives in your country. How the hell are you ever going to find him, or be found by him? The odds are really prohibitive—worse than winning the lottery.

Do we have to accept this grim vision? I don't think so. The notion of the one and only Mr. Right is a myth, invented to overheat your brain, to derail your quest for happiness. If you are hoodwinked into believing that there is only one man out there for you, you will have a tendency to either

- get discouraged and settle for less, thinking you'll never find him;
- give up and live alone;
- wrongly assume that the first guy who shows up carrying flowers is Mr. Right. The tendency to over-romanticize a man who makes a decent effort to woo you in an old-fashioned way is one of the most common mistakes that women make with men. And the myth of the one-and-only Mr. Right plays right into this.

And another thing: If only one man is meant for you, who meant him? Who had the audacity to decide which man was right for you? The most common answer to this question is, "Destiny." (Or Cupid, or maybe Dr. Phil.) Or are these love matches just "meant to be" in some cosmic, impersonal way... written in the stars. That is so romantic, isn't it?

Let's stick with Destiny. It's time to blow out the scented candles, and look at the Destiny myth in the cold light of day. Let's assume that Destiny is a real person, a rosy-cheeked old codger with a long white beard who, long ago, wrote up your perfect match in the Book of Fate. Fine. But if Destiny chose Mr. Right for you, why hasn't Destiny taken care of a few other details, like making sure you *meet* your true love? Destiny controls everything, according to the theory. Look around you. Does it look as if most people ever meet their perfect love? So what did this grand selection really accomplish? Apparently the guy is asleep at the wheel.

The other thing that is wrong with the Destiny theory is this. It takes credit for *everything*, even your own initiative and hard work.

Let's consider an example of Destiny at work.

Apparently Destiny is asleep at the wheel.

Sam was a writer of historical novels who took advantage of paid research trips to search the world for his perfect mate, using every technique known to man. He went to many countries, he hung out where interesting women hang out. He never wasted time on shallow attraction. And at last he found her at a wine tasting in Macon, France. Sam found Elaine: Now they live happily together with three kids in New Jersey. Elaine is the love of his life. Ask her how she met him. "It was Destiny," she sighs. Well sure. I guess it must have been destined that Sam would work that hard on his quest. And because he did, he found her.

You see the problem? *Whatever* happens is destined! Including major *efforts* that lead to *results*. Yet people persist in thinking, "I might as well not make any effort, 'cause Destiny is in charge here."

Destiny is really just another version of what the philosophers call *determinism*—the view that the future is already fixed. When people first encounter this idea, they often heave a sad sigh and say, "Gee, if it's all decided in advance, why should I try at anything?" What they fail to consider is that even given this theory, all the *trying* that goes on, which often affects the outcome, must be determined too. So you are still stuck with the same decisions, and challenges, as before.

The truth is, the Destiny concept of romance just strips you of power. If Destiny has chosen your mate, you become a pawn in the game. Little-old-you can't know what Destiny knows! Destiny is an expert, with authority! You couldn't be expected to know what would make *you* happy...

Or could you?

We want so badly to believe in perfection. That is what sucks us in. If some higher power has chosen the one for us, then that someone will be perfect for us. If we can just stumble onto that person then we can live in a fairytale. Bring on the eternal bliss. Then we don't have to be realistic, we can just sit helplessly by in a sort of romantic stupor, like Sleeping Beauty waiting for her prince, depending on inscrutable forces to serve up happiness if and when they see fit. We don't have to admit the real truth—that no mate is perfect.

Earth to you—are you perfect? Then why would your man be? Even the luckiest couples sometimes quarrel, sometimes are sad, sometimes feel distant, sometimes get bored with each other. (But they recover, and they don't inflict needless pain on each other, and they walk on, hand in hand in the real world.)

Consider what this means. It means that some men are worse, and some are better—it's a matter of degree—and your job is to identify the best candidates you can. Also, and most importantly, there will be *many of them*, not just one.

This news cuts both ways. On the minus side, it means you have some work to do, and there is no one right answer, no mystic absolute to cling to. On the plus side, it means your odds are suddenly much better. There are a whole bunch of guys out there, any one of whom would make a great mate for you, and your job is to meet one of these men who is up to your standards and truly compatible, and then get on with it. Let love develop with that person.

Once your love develops, he will _become_ the only one for you. That is what _attachment_ means. It is your heart, not Destiny, that turns a mere man into a unique, irreplaceable partner for all your days.

This may seem too cold, not romantic enough. But what could be more romantic than ending up half of a happy couple? The fire will be just as warm, the couch just as cozy, the roses just as fragrant, when you ditch Destiny and go out and find yourself a good man. (Or make it possible for him to find you.)

BEFORE YOU CAN MATE, YOU HAVE TO MEET

The Underrated Chance Encounter

*M*eeting in person is the old-fashioned way, nature's way, and humans are designed to be able to tell a whole lot the first time they stand face to face with a new person. Do I mean that love at first sight is actually possible? Read on.

Meanwhile I *will* say this: I wish that simpatico people met more often. I wish that without trying, you could encounter lots and lots of eligible men, until you found a good one for you and could get on with being happy.

Later I will explore ways you can improve the odds by putting yourself in situations where you're more likely to meet a suitable guy. But before I do that, let's give some credit to a type of meeting that is too often overlooked: the chance encounter. The total accident.

Opportunities with huge potential come along more often than you may realize.

THE CHANCE ENCOUNTER

There's no doubt that we would all rather meet an interesting new person when we are at our best. Wearing a nice ensemble, hair just right, well-rested, unstressed, and with the kind of minty breath that leads to happiness on TV commercials.

And we're more likely to be at our best when meeting someone is on the agenda.

But life doesn't always go that way.

Let's say it's a rainy Wednesday. After work you drove home through gridlock, changed into something comfortable, fed the cat. Now you remember that you promised yourself to occasionally eat some fruit and vegetables. But the fridge is bare.

Five minutes later you run into the grocery store, in your sweats, with your hair tied up in a shape resembling an extinct bird. (Unbeknownst to you, you look pretty hot that way.) You are in the produce section, trying to choose a good apple.

A man is nearby. You get the feeling he has noticed you.

You continue what you are doing, and you see him again, dawdling by the mandarin oranges. You catch him looking at you. You give him a once over and you decide that he is attractive. He seems intelligent, judging by the nice selection of romaine, arugula, and cherry tomatoes in his cart. His fingers are ringless. His jeans fit.

Then what happens?

Do you make eye contact, or do you avoid it?

Do you smile at him?

Do you speak to him?

Do you think, "He's appalled by my rubber-band scrunchie" or, "Maybe I remind him of someone"?

Do you think, "Oh-oh, a stalker. Better hightail it"?

Do you think, "When I lose that twenty pounds, I'll come back here and maybe I'll see him"?

Does it occur to you, "I am always complaining that I never meet men; I could probably meet this man"?

If so, do you think of thirty-five excuses not to?

Does anything happen?

Do you *want* anything to happen?

After all, this is not an Official Meeting Occasion. You aren't dressed. You are a Highly Organized Professional, and this is not a time slot that you had allotted to the purpose of encountering anyone. Who cares if this guy looks like a better prospect than all the men you had intentional meetings with in the last ten years?

If a man speaks to a woman standing by the Braeburn apples, she is quite likely to rebuff him.

Who cares? I do. It is my considered opinion that some of the best mates are ones you won't ever meet if you are too structured in your approach. Men are not so rigid: They often see the chance, and hanker after it. But they are cowards, they are cautious; they wait too long, trying to think of a good line, and the opportunity slips away. If a man does screw up his courage in time, and speaks to a woman standing by the Braeburn apples, she is quite likely to rebuff him—because she doesn't see this as an appropriate place to meet a new person. Her head is full of objections, like the ones I listed a moment ago.

Our heroine should resist these negative voices. She should consider that she may not run into this fellow again. If her gut says he is interesting, then maybe he is. Which leads us to another axiom:

Any time is a good time to meet Mr. Right.

The thing is, it doesn't do you any good to be ready for a Vogue cover shot if the guy you're talking to is a dud. But conversely, if a guy who does look like a contender is showing obvious interest in you, then it doesn't matter that you had no chance to plan your outfit for him; *he already likes you.* All you have to do is not reject him. Just be friendly, give him a chance, and explore the situation. It takes very little interaction to determine whether you might like to see this person again. If you don't, you've lost nothing. If you do, that can be arranged.

In short, the best opportunities don't always come with labels. You have to recognize them. And be brave enough to act on them.

Nor do you have to just wait passively for such encounters to happen. They don't have to be so "chance-y." You can seek out situations where chance encounters are more likely to occur.

Certain venues are more conducive to something positive happening. In some venues, people feel freer. More open. More optimistic. More sure of their ground. In a moment, I will take a look at the features of a good meeting place, and will rate the common sites where men and women run into each other.

But first I need to investigate something more basic: the ways in which males and females evaluate and choose each other. You may not totally approve of what I have to say about this. But it might just ring a few bells.

I will begin with the male.

3

HOW MEN CHOOSE WOMEN

The Concept of a Sighting

*F*irst let me say, I don't mean to imply that men get to do the choosing. It isn't like a vegetable stand, where a man can say, "I'll take this pepper here, not these others," and the pepper has nothing to say about it. What I'm talking about is how men pick out which women they are going to *try* for.

Let's face it, men are loons. They have their own ways of doing things. They don't proceed in a politically correct, enlightened way to select their woman. They may end up valuing her for the right things, the things she wants to be valued for; but that is not always how they start.

Men are hard-wired to look for certain features. Evolution wants the mating process to succeed, and so it makes sure that men home in on that which will be conducive to success, regardless of how unrefined this strategy may be.

But no matter how strange men are, if you want to meet the right man you have to clue in to how men think. (Okay, "think" may be a bit of a stretch.) If you try to change men or just don't get them, you'll be stymied—but if you accept how they are and forgive them and work with them, you will have enormous power and effectiveness.

Men want to look. First, foremost, and always, men are visual. Men's eyes are always wandering, seeking out that which they could and would impregnate. Why is this so, Mr. Darwin? "Well, it's because the genes that triggered that kind of behaviour survived the best, down through the ages, until all the men who were left had those genes." In other words, an obsession with reproduction leads to a better reproductive score...or something...let's not get too technical. The fact is men can't help shopping with the eyes, even happily married men, even old codgers who think Viagra is better than money.

So the first rule is, *let men see you.* This may seem too obvious to even mention, but it is the key to the whole thing. If you make it difficult to be seen—for instance, if you sit in the back booth with shades on—you stop Step One from happening. So none of the other steps can. (Being seen is particularly crucial, and achievable, if you are trying to meet Mr. Right online. More about that later.)

WHAT MEN ARE LOOKING FOR

Now let us ask, what are men looking for? What are they hoping to see? If you're feeling cynical, your answer may be, "Cameron Diaz." Or if you happen to look like Cameron Diaz, your equally discouraged answer may be, "Keira Knightly." But this is so wrong it is laughable.

Men are, in the first place, looking for *attractive.* You might think you know exactly what that means. But you might be wrong. The good news is, attractive means completely different things to different men.

Different men like completely different bodies.

Many men in our culture like slender, athletic female figures—some men really do, and some just say they do, because they are ashamed of admitting anything else to their male peer group. Some men may want the rail-thin model type. But many men in our culture do not want a slender woman: They want someone with more generous curves. Some men like pear-shaped women; some men like inverted pears. And some men don't really care that much about body size or shape.

Our evolving male has tried, with those few cells in his brain devoted to self-knowledge, to wrestle with this question.

Then we have faces. Here there is even less consensus. No one agrees on faces. A face that strikes one man as masculine may seem feminine to another. A face that strikes Tom as sexy may look shallow to Harry. Ralph may hate a lot of makeup on a woman, while Shawn considers it a turn-on. There are no objective standards concerning faces. Even in the realm of extremely good-looking celebrities, you will find a whole gamut of opinions. I know men who think Britney Spears is homely. I know men who think Pamela Anderson is grotesque.

I know men who dislike all blondes. Men who dislike brunettes. Men who appreciate a good tan. Men who adore very pale skin. Boob men. Leg men. I knew a guy who got very turned on by a woman's handshake if it was "as strong as a man's"! (His friends told him he was in the closet, but he stuck to his guns.)

All this may strike the sensitive, intelligent woman as very superficial, even offensive. "How shallow can guys get?" you may ask. Surely the cultured, educated, spiritual (yet masculine) man of *your* dreams doesn't look only at the outside of a woman.

"True beauty is on the inside," women cry out from the salons of the world. "Besides," I hear them say, "We women are forgiving of men's looks—why can't men return the favour?"

The scientists say that men and women are both designed to be ruthlessly pragmatic in their criteria for a mate. Women are programmed by evolution to choose men based on their fathering potential, which is closely associated with status in the group—what we now call money and power. Men, regardless of their conscious attitude towards having kids, are designed to look for good reproducers. A low waist-to-hip ratio of seven to ten signifies that a woman is likely to be a success at bearing children. (Larger waists relative to the hips have been linked to lower estrogen levels, less body fat available to sustain pregnancy, and lower fertility.) And in both sexes, facial beauty is associated with grace, intelligence, popularity, and, in general, fitness for survival.

So forget about how superficial men may be and realize that they, like you, are hard-wired in mysterious ways, which may not be as shallow as you think. (And fortunately, lots of men don't toe the evolutionary line in every way—apparently their wiring has come loose.)

Take faces, for example. It's clear that we read far more in a face than looks. We think we are reading souls. We look into the eyes of the person we are talking to, and we feel as if we can tell who they are, deep down—what they value, what they love. With certain people, something about the face feels familiar, even familial. Many people strike us as somehow alien; but some faces arouse in us a strange empathy from the first time we set eyes on them.

What is a man doing when he looks at you? On some level, quite possibly unconscious, he is (or his genes are) probably trying to decide, could this person be a lover or is she just a potential friend? If the answer comes up "lover," his charm will probably kick in, and there will be a lot of twinkling eyes and banter and smiling (read: spreading of plumage) that might not take place if his circuits decided on "friend." And how is the decision made? Let's assume he finds you to be above some basic threshold of attractiveness—what other factors come into play?

Well, as odd as it may sound, you are being checked out in a number of ways to determine whether you are *too intimidating*. You are being studied to see whether you are likely to defeat him as a lover. I mean this in the most literal way: He wants to know whether in your presence he might be *unable to perform*.

The average male who is old enough and mature enough to want to marry, has realized that sex is not always a triumph. I'm not saying he is sexually insecure: Indeed, with the right woman he may be easygoing, studly, and confident. But therein lies the rub. How does he know which women are "right"?

Our evolving male has tried, with those few cells in his brain devoted to self-knowledge, to wrestle with this question. This has made him attentive to factors that influence his chemistry with women. Many of these factors are hard to pin down: Who knows what creates that magical heat between some pairs of people? Who has bravely catalogued the qualities of particular women that threaten his ego, and thereby his arousal? But one area, at least, seems to be a no-brainer: his own physical likes and dislikes. So he tries to screen out anything that might lessen his prowess if he were invited to perform.

This isn't all selfish. When a man spies a woman who is really "his type"—*whatever* this may be—he thinks he has found someone whose sexual needs he could enthusiastically fulfill. Shall we blame him for thinking this is good news for her too?

Intimidation and Attraction: A Vignette

It's lunchtime. Randy and Tom find themselves sitting next to a rather elegant woman in a bar/restaurant in the business district. They strike up a conversation while waiting for their respective tables. The woman, Rachel, is friendly, glad to have someone to talk to while she waits for a friend to show up. The men are responding in kind, but meanwhile they are both, as discreetly as they can, checking Rachel out.

Now it happens that Rachel, though strikingly attractive, has a slightly hawk-like cast to her features, a fierceness built into her face that reads *to Randy* as intimidating, and as a bit masculine. He senses in her an unswerving confidence in herself and in the cosmos, and a capacity for aggression, that make him feel he may be out of his league. So Randy is leaning towards a no on the lover issue, except for one thing: He has noticed that Rachel (who is wearing an attractive taupe business suit) has long, very good legs, and Randy is a confirmed leg man. (He is having trouble getting views of her legs, because he is right next to her, and has to lean back and tilt his head to inspect them.) To make matters worse, Rachel has said she is a defence attorney. Randy is a tax lawyer, and they are bantering about the legal scene. But he opted out of court work because it was too scary, and he is very conscious of a threat to his ego in this woman. Those legs make him wish that she didn't intimidate him, but he can't fight the verdict of his genes.

Meanwhile Tom, who is one barstool over, is caught in a different struggle. Tom does not perceive Rachel as hawk-like or aggressive; he came from a family of women who had features somewhat like Rachel's, and to him her face represents not only beauty, but also comfort, femininity, and warmth. Tom is half in love already. He is not an attorney and is not directly threatened by any status Rachel may have in that area. Tom's problem is that he can't seem to get into the conversation (Randy is next to Rachel and they are talking shop), and is therefore unable to tell how he and Rachel might get along, or even how she might react to him. Tom is divorced, has been lonely and horny for ages, and he has checked Rachel's hand and found no ring.

Tom has one other problem. Tom prefers full-figured women. Whether he likes it or not, his sexual confidence is tied to the Rubenesque shape: He becomes just a little unsure without it—riper curves are the catalyst that sparks his sexual chemistry. So ever since he noticed how lovely Rachel is, Tom has been trying to lean around his stocky friend Randy and get a gander at Rachel's body. But Randy is always in the way, and unfortunately Rachel is wearing a business suit and the jacket pretty much hides her shape.

Just as the men's table is announced, two things happen. Rachel says to Randy, "The only place that really matters to me is our family cottage on the lake," and Rachel twists towards them on her stool, her jacket falls open, and Tom has his first unobstructed view of the generous curve of her chest in a crème blouse. Tom is now completely smitten, because his own sacred place happens to be a cottage on a lake, and he is absolutely clear that physically, Rachel is his wet dream.

This woman is elegant, she is smart, and she cares about lakes.

Tom now has achieved what I call in this book a "sighting." Tom is beside himself, if you must know the truth. Behind his exterior calm he is hyperventilating, because this *never happens*. He knows right now, with the same certainty that he knows his own address, that he could be happy with this woman.

This never happens. He sees women whom he finds attractive, sometimes, but they are not alone. And they are usually married. Mostly he sees them across a room or across the street. And he never gets to hear them talk about their lives, never gets even a hint as to whether he might be compatible with them in a personal sense. On this occasion in the restaurant, all of these sad rules have found an exception.

This woman is elegant, she is smart, and she cares about lakes. And in Tom's eyes, she is a goddess.

Randy gets up to go to their table. He says goodbye to Rachel, who gives him a warm smile. Tom suspects that Rachel is attracted to Randy. Tom has no sense at all of Rachel even noticing him. He smiles at her but his smile comes out anxious and stiff, because for him there is too much at stake and he has no cards to play. Randy says, "Let's go, bud," a little sarcastically, and Tom realizes he is just standing there in a haze, gazing at Rachel. Randy tugs him away and says to Rachel, "This guy needs to eat."

Tom flushes and follows Randy into the restaurant area, and they order. Randy says dismissively, "She was nice, but kind of butch looking. A little hefty, too." Tom, who knows his own taste for fuller figured women is atypical of his male peer group, keeps quiet. He doesn't mention that he just lost the love of his life. A few minutes later, they see Rachel sit down in a nearby booth with a very good-looking, well dressed man, who seems to be locked in constant hilarity with her. Tom abandons a half-formed plan of somehow talking to her before heading back to work.

And there you have it, a typical session in the endless male search. What can be learned from it? Let's inventory a few useful points:

- Facial looks are totally subjective: The same woman can look feminine and pretty to one man and just the opposite to another. The same goes for body shapes and sizes.
- Total accidents of seating and attitude can stop major connections from being made.
- Men very rarely have positive sightings, and usually are not in a position to act even on those.
- Men's relentless scrutiny of women, the thing that drives feminists crazy, is just as much *a screening out of that which is intimidating* as it is a judging of whether someone is up to par. If truth be known, Randy's dismissal of Rachel had little to do with her being not pretty enough or too heavy. These were excuses. The truth is, he found her intimidating as a lawyer and as a woman.
- The most confident, forward man in the group is not always the most interested one. He may be confident because he isn't interested, and therefore has nothing to lose. The one who can't get a word out may be the one who is stricken with attraction.
- Qualities of character are often in play from the beginning: Men may seem to be judging solely on appearance— but in fact they see *in appearance* many other levels of humanity. In Rachel's face, Tom saw warmth, love of family, kindness, intelligence. In her words he heard a love for a type of sacred place that he too values. Even her body's sexual appeal to him held other levels of connection—in her full figure he saw a comforting quality, and a sensual opulence, that spoke to his emotional needs. (Randy saw qualities of mind that scared him off.) Both men were reacting to a whole person, through her appearance.

And what did Rachel think?

Here we encounter an amazing disparity—a gap like the Grand Canyon. Her experience was so unlike that of the men as to seem like a cruel cosmic joke. Rachel did not have "finding a man" on her agenda. She wanted to meet her friend Pete and have lunch, and she was preoccupied with a trial she is in the middle of. Pete works at the same firm she does, and they hang out together a lot, but there is no chemistry between them and that is why they have the relaxed, hilarious rapport that Tom noticed later.

Rachel broke up with a long-term lover six months ago when she discovered he was cheating on her. Although she is lonely and occasionally makes a slight effort to meet new people, she is sceptical of all men. And anyway, *she does not think of a bar as a place where she could ever meet a man.* She was perfectly happy to talk to Randy, but did not even ask herself whether he was relationship material—he was just a fellow lawyer. Tom she hardly noticed. She did observe that he had a nice face, but it never occurred to her for a moment that he was interested in her; and he seemed sort of uptight and sad compared to his friend.

There is no chemistry between them and that is why they have a relaxed, hilarious rapport.

Rachel's attitude to her body is even more tragically counterproductive. Rachel has regretted since about age sixteen that she is not skinnier. She thinks of herself as heavy, because although she has a model's legs, she has rounded hips and a full bosom. Actually, she thinks she's fat. If she could only lose thirty pounds, she might be acceptable in her own eyes. She has an older sister who still weighs 115 pounds and this torments her daily. Somewhere inside her a voice still says, "You're beautiful," but lately she has had trouble hearing it.

Oh, Rachel! The truth is, you have a classic hourglass figure, and many men would find you almost overwhelmingly sexy if you would let them—and if they could escape the caustic stereotypes of their peer group. It certainly never occurred to Rachel that Tom is a man who absolutely cherishes the very body type that she represents, at the weight where she is. Or that her jacket was preventing such an admirer from even verifying that she is what he admires!

Tom, a man who is normally cheerful and entertaining, managed only to seem a bit sad to her.

And if he seemed sad, maybe he had a right to be.

Because something sad did just happen.

Rachel just walked away from Mr. Right. Tom was it.

Don't get me wrong here: I am not saying that Rachel did anything wrong. Though she could be accused of being somewhat unaware. In fact her assumptions meant that she was, in effect, *asleep to the possibility* that was right next to her.

Unfortunately, near misses like this happen all the time. People who would be perfect together pass like the proverbial ships in the night. Then they trudge on down life's path, forever lonely. Women cruise through situations, blissfully unaware of the life-and-death struggle going on in the man who is right next to them.

For it *is* a life-and-death struggle. Biologically, nothing is more important than successful mating. And for an average male who is old enough and mature enough to want to marry, that challenge is an awesome test, a labour of Hercules, fraught with perils and obstacles. The main peril is rejection (intensified by the competition of other males, many of whom have him beaten in one way or another—looks, money, physique, smarts, style, confidence...). The main obstacle is rarity: Too seldom does our eligible male encounter an unattached and approachable female who he senses could really be the one.

No wonder a man goes a little crazy when a true sighting happens—success and happiness and an end to loneliness are beckoning to him, if he can only make the right moves. In my example, Tom froze up completely, even managed to make himself *less* attractive! Became stiff and sad-looking, tongue-tied.

Must we leave my little story of the yuppie lovers, with a bad ending? Could Rachel have done anything to change the outcome?

Well, suppose we replay the scene with just a few tiny changes. This time, Rachel keeps it in mind that any place is a good place to meet Mr. Right.

Let's say that again. *Any place is a good place to meet Mr. Right.*

This time she isn't asleep: She has her antennae switched on. Then she may well notice that lawyer Randy is not really interested in her. And that he is a bit of a bore—too needy in the ego department. And she may well pick up on the fact that Tom is eyeing her in an almost stressed way. Why is he doing that? Maybe he fancies her. Maybe she should make a point to speak to him, instead of letting this insecure tax attorney hog all her time. Tom does have a very nice face, after all. So she leans across Randy, smiles at Tom, realizes that her jacket has fallen open, which is fine, and says to Tom, "Why do you hang out with this lawyer boy, anyway? Can't you do any better?"

Tom lights up at this suggestion that she has noticed him, at her sense of humour, and at the curves that he has just detected. Tom starts to talk to her; Randy decides to go to the restroom; Tom cannot resist moving over next to her. They discover their mutual love of lakes and cottages. He asks her if she is meeting someone for lunch. She says yes, but he's just a friend. Finally Tom cannot restrain himself. He asks for her card. She gives it to him. They smile at each other. Love is born.

(Somewhere, Cupid watches with furrowed brow. That mischievous imp specializes in creating chemistry between the wrong people. So he frowns, because two souls who will be happy together have found each other.)

4

HOW WOMEN CHOOSE MEN

Or, What You Don't Always Admit

*W*omen say that they don't choose men based on looks, so it is unfair that men subject them to this harsh treatment. There is some truth to this statement, but not as much as you might assume.

I was sitting with my friend Marsha in a bar. We were people-watching and chatting and eating some calamari. She had been surveying all the men in our vicinity. Then she sighed, "Why is it so hard to find any attractive men in this town?"

I looked around. I saw a tired businessman who seemed okay, a guy reading poetry who looked kind of bohemian, two jocks staring at the silent TV. How did Marsha know that none of these guys was "attractive"?

Apparently she could tell, just by looking, that these guys didn't attract her. "You see," I said, "looks do matter!"

"It isn't looks. I don't care if they are handsome or not..."

"Well, it may not be *looks*, but it is something you are *seeing*, no?"

The problem is that "looks" could mean "whether someone is good-looking," or it could mean "what you learn when you look at someone." We all rely on visual perception to tell us a whole lot about the people we encounter. Very little of it has to do with how stereotypically good-looking they are.

Here are some of the things we detect:

Style. What a great word. What a slippery concept. Marsha examined the tired businessman. "What's wrong with him?" I asked.

"He's too polyester." Okay, that makes sense. Those shiny pants don't attract her. The jacket looks cheap, the tie is cliché. She sees no originality there. She sees a guy who probably uses too much of the wrong cologne. She sees someone who wears a shirt and tie out of necessity, but finds no joy in clothes. She sees a drone.

"He doesn't care about superficial things like regular bathing."

Hygiene. What about the guy reading poetry in the corner, at a window table by himself? Marsha is always saying that she wants a man who is into the arts, who cares about culture. That guy is reading Philip Larkin's *Collected Poems*, for god's sake. Marsha leans over to me and says, "I just know he would have bad personal habits. He doesn't care about superficial things like regular bathing."

I say, "That's ridiculous. How can you know that?"

She says, "Trust me. Look at his hair. It's scruffy. He looks like the early Dylan."

And so it goes. Admittedly, the sweater he has on is a bit ratty. And his teeth don't look terrific. But what does she want from a bohemian?

Intelligence. Marsha doesn't dig the two jocks under the TV. They have longish hair crushed by baseball caps. They are slapping each other and guffawing. They are loud. One of them is quite handsome. I point that out. "He's stupid," she says. "Look at the cartoon he's laughing at. I don't do stupid."

Then a guy sits down next to us. He looks smart and clean and rather cool in an unstudied way. Could he be the perfect guy? "He's, like, 5′ 5″ in boots!" she whispers to me in horror.

"Only the inside matters," women say. "Qualities of character float my boat."

But just let him be 5′ 10″, at least. Or how can I ever wear heels? And let him be the teddy bear type. Or not. Let him have a hairy chest like Sean Connery. In fact, let him look in every way like Sean Connery. Only with hair instead of a hairpiece. And thirty years younger. Or not. Let him have a nice butt. Broad shoulders. Strong hands.

The list could go on. And on. You look at a stranger, and you see things. You see attitude. Class background. Ancestry. Fitness. Health. Personality type. Openness. Empathy. Conservativeness or liberality. Uptightness or easygoingness. Professionalism or counterculture-ism. Artificiality or naturalness. You see soul, or think you don't see it. You see someone you can relate to, someone who seems akin to yourself—or you see a barrier. Even if you don't care whether he is good-looking (and the truth is, this does interest you), there is so much to see. So much. Women are even more astute than men in picking up all this complex information, *just by looking*.

Surprise. Women are visual too.

And when men think they are looking to see if someone is good-looking or sexy, the truth is, they are picking up a lot of this other stuff too (as we saw in the previous chapter).

And guess what? You can catch this kind of information in a photo too. A good photo will tell you volumes about the person in it. That is why if you meet a man online or through a print or telephone ad, you are right to ask for a photo from the get-go. I don't think anyone really knows why Jack is attracted to Jill, or vice versa. It probably isn't about looks, but much of it can be seen anyway, and can be revealed in a photograph. Lots of times you will see a photo of someone and immediately know you wouldn't do well together—whether they are drop-dead gorgeous or not.

What about face and body, in a purely aesthetic sense? Well, it has to be admitted that women are often more forgiving in their requirements than men like to think men are. (I said "often;" I said "like to think.") Men, especially when they are out with other men, like to critique women in a merciless fashion, like judges at a beauty contest; but look at your average husband and wife with a long-lasting marriage and you will see a different story. Go to a dance hall where real couples go because they actually like to dance. Take a hard look at the specimens in front of you. The fact is, most people get pudgier as they get older. And most people aren't that good-looking to begin with. As you ease into middle age, you may observe that most of the good-looking people around you have something in common: They are young.

As you get a little older and wiser, you realize even this isn't quite right. The real truth is, youth is easily mistaken for beauty. Younger people have firmer skin, more energy, less fat, less emotional baggage showing in their faces and bodies. That can make them seem as if they are good-looking. But in fact, one of the tests of real beauty is that it tends to survive time's ravages. When a face has a truly great design, that fact endures. Think how often actors with movie star looks age badly. Looking at Jack Nicholson now, are you tempted to praise the beauty of his face? Does he not look as if his massive brow shifted, or slipped, down over his eyes and nearly eradicated them? Looking back, you see that he had charm and zest and a great smile—and youth, youth, youth. But even in his early pictures you can see that his face wasn't well constructed—the brow was already threatening to slump down over the eyes.

Then look at older people like Catherine Deneuve or Cary Grant or Stephanie Powers or our old friend Sean Connery—now that is real facial beauty; and that is rare.

Most of us are not at that height. Most married couples have found something else to value more than looks—and the men have found it as well as the women.

Let him have a hairy chest like Sean Connery. In fact, let him look in every way like Sean Connery.

So although men are visual and women are visual too, looks are not the biggest issue here. When you and your Mr. Right see each other, you will both see much more than what is on the surface. So whether or not you would give yourself a high score in the classical-beauty department, you should not hesitate to give yourself a chance to see and be seen by desirable men. Which brings us to our next topic.

5

THE PERFECT PLACE TO MEET

The ideal venue for you to meet a man should possess as many as possible of the following characteristics:

Visual access. In the ideal venue you can see the other person, and he can see you. Online fails this test; so do telephone networks. But even in those cases, the problem can be worked around, as we shall see. (Even if you think you don't care all that much whether you can see the guy you are considering, rest assured that visual data helps us function naturally.)

Approachability. In the ideal venue you can speak to a stranger without feeling pushy or forward or awkward. And he has the same freedom to speak to you. Ideally, people are circulating and mingling, and that is the very nature of the venue. The problem with most places for meeting someone is that they lack this characteristic. In most public places, people do not feel comfortable approaching strangers and speaking to them. Oddly enough, online and telephone networks pass this test: They afford graceful ways of introducing oneself to a new person.

Pleasant, comfortable surroundings. Not dingy, not smoky, not dangerous. (If you like being at home and can't be bothered with clothes, the Internet again scores high on this test.)

It offers people you're comfortable with. If you are an urban professional with several degrees who came from an upper middle-class family, check out places where such as you gather. (The reason for this is not snobbery: It goes deeper than that—see Chapter 18.) If you are a sun and beer person who likes the throb of a Harley under you, get with those folks to find the perfect mate. Good pubs, of course, usually offer a cross-section of people, a richer mixture that you can't go wrong with. More about that later.

Failure does not have fatal consequences. Meaning, this is the sort of situation where, if the relationship goes bad, you're still okay. Your work place may not score high in this respect.

Think for a moment: What place has all these virtues?

PRIVATE PARTIES: IF ONLY…

Think of a great private party. Maybe it's in an old house, the kind with big windows and pine floors and high ceilings. In an older part of town, but the neighbourhood is rising again. The place is crawling with people; a few too many is about right. There is music in one room, maybe some dancing, but plenty of rooms have just the sound of chatter. People throng in the kitchen, hot food is being prepped. Some guests know each other, but many don't, new blood is circulating. It's noisy, a bit crazy. Anyone can talk to anyone, without the slightest feeling of being intrusive.

You walk in, you wander, you joke with different people, you roam around and case the whole joint. There are plenty of unattached people. You run into friends, who introduce new people to you. This is key, of course. But you can also just smile at someone you've never seen before and end up in a huddle with him for hours.

It seems that college kids, and recent grads, are constantly thrown into situations like this. No wonder they have no trouble finding dates!

That is the problem with private parties. There just aren't enough to go around.

Yes, private parties are the best place to meet a mate. They are a social mechanism proven by tradition, a graceful, happy way of honouring the need that most of us have to encounter new people. And to look them over before wading in. If you are lucky enough to be part of a social set that mixes married and single people, that throws a lot of parties, that constantly takes care to add new folks to the mix—then congratulations, because you are probably not alone, and on top of that, you are probably either young or rich or both.

Because that is the problem with private parties. There just aren't enough to go around. In today's fragmented urban society, many people seldom get invited to such a thing. Or if they do, it turns out to be that worst of all fates, a suburban private party. (The unhappy guests gather in a house in the suburbs, far from stores, cafés, and other signs of life. All but three guests are married. And one of those three is gay. Everyone knows everyone. All the women look stressed out. The guys are all more capable of looming near beer coolers or televisions with the game on than of conversing. No one meets anyone new. This is not a party, it's a wake for dead social lives.)

If you do have a chance to go to a *good* private party, or several of them, go. Enjoy yourself, and remember that this is the perfect place for meeting a good man. Don't spend the whole evening talking to people you already know. Be an explorer. Of course, that only gets you launched. Major questions still arise. (How do you tell Mr. Right from Mr. Wrong? How do you act if you find a possible Mr. Right? And so on.)

No matter where you meet him, these questions will arise. And I will answer them, all of them, later.

In the meantime: Where else is he hiding?

THE DINNER PARTY: A RARE BREED

Well, of course there is the deluxe version of the private party, something known as the *dinner party*. Now really, this is the finest thing society offers, but is even more rare than the private party. A dinner party is a bunch of people sitting around a table, not too many. They have all been invited, they are in someone's home, and they ideally don't all know each other before this occasion. Best of all, at a good dinner party only one person talks at a time, and everyone else listens to that person. Everyone is participating in the same conversation.

"Do such things still go on?" you ask. Well, admittedly this type of gathering is a rare and endangered beast. No cell phones. No TV. Plenty of opportunity for wit, for storytelling, for sharing of experiences.

The problem is the odds. If you are lucky enough to find yourself at such a get-together, you probably know most of the folks there. What are the chances that among the rest is an unattached guy who fits your bill? Not good. But if Mr. Single Right Guy is there, you are in luck—a dinner party is a perfect place to notice and be noticed, to begin a friendship, to strike sparks in total style and safety.

You could, of course, throw your own dinner party, and ask your guests to bring "interesting strangers." You could create the ideal venue right in your own home.

Where else? We'll tackle the obvious one—bars—last. There are lots of other viable venues.

ON THE JOB

Much has been written and said about how unwise (unprofessional/unethical) it is to date people you meet on the job. But the urban lifestyle is tough, lonely, and isolating. Try living in LA. Most people in LA are either asleep, at home watching the tube, in their car, or at work. Sleeping, driving, and watching TV are not the best ways to meet new friends, so that leaves work. People meet other people at work. Often they work in big corporations, and encounter a lot of people. And guess what: This is where their friends come from. And for better or worse, some of these friends turn into lovers.

Sleeping with a co-worker is fine until you get caught necking in the stairwell by the CEO.

In fact, the workplace is not a bad setting in which to observe another person. In that stressful environment there are many chances to demonstrate weakness or strength, to behave kindly or brutally. You can watch how someone treats his superiors, and how he treats the folks he supervises. That last point is crucial: Beware the man who abuses, condescends to, or neglects his underlings. Watch out for those who are reluctant to share information with their helpers. Steer clear of those who butter up their bosses, and then bad-mouth them behind their backs.

Yes, you can use the workplace as a lab in which to detect qualities of character that matter in a mate. And you can strike up an acquaintance with almost anyone without feeling out of line. Recall my criteria for a good venue: visual access, approachability, pleasant surroundings, people you're comfortable with. The workplace doesn't look too shabby, does it?

Unfortunately there is criterion number five: Consequences of failure.

The trouble with sleeping with a co-worker is that it's fine until

- others hear about it, and start gossiping,
- you get caught necking in the stairwell by the CEO,
- the affair goes bad.

That last point may be the worst. It is very unpleasant to be forced to work with someone with whom you are having a romantic tiff—or worse, when one of you has dumped the other. Particularly if one supervises the other. This can create opportunities for revenge and/or blackmail that are terrifying to contemplate.

If, however, you meet someone interesting during your work day (or at lunch) who is *not part of the same chain of command* (or even the same corporation) that you belong to, it may be fine to pursue the chance. If you don't have to work together, and neither of you has supervisory power over the other, go for it. With one obvious exception: If there is a client relationship on either side, steer clear.

The bottom line here is this: The workplace is a very good venue in which to run into the same person regularly, and to observe and evaluate him without any risk whatsoever before taking the plunge of seeing him one-on-one. If you start having the occasional lunch with him, this can be a low-pressure, pleasant way to embark on a friendship, and later on, to decide whether the friendship wants to be more than platonic. Given how many people we meet in the working world, and how few we meet elsewhere, you would be a fool *not* to be open to good prospects that appear on your radar screen.

BOOKSTORES AND LIBRARIES

If you are a literate, well-read person, it is imperative that you find a guy who is the same. In my chapter on compatibility, I look at the reasons why. For now, take my word for it: *Do not dream for a moment that you will end up happy with a man who isn't your intellectual match.*

What better place to run into men who actually like books, than a bookstore? (And libraries are not only cool, but sexy too.)

Especially practical are today's lavish book emporia. The big chains have gotten smart and realized that people who stay longer buy more. Free reading does not discourage book buying; eventually, like cave persons, we want to drag our prize home. So we get bookstores with tables and chairs and couches and a Starbucks adjoining.

These "second homes" can be an ideal place to encounter a mate.

Of course, it is tricky. You can't just roam through the aisles looking for a guy with nice buns. Well, you can. But you probably won't.

More likely, it may happen like this. You will be standing in front of the self-help section, wondering if you should reread *Chicken Soup for the Macramé-making Soul*. You glance around and you notice that a guy sitting on a nearby bench is leafing through *Chicken Soup for the Scuba Diving Soul*. This is a

Excuse me. If he looks at you, you

dead give-away: He likes the same family of books that you do. Give him a quick look-over. If any positive bells ring, if your genes seem to vibrate at all, you should wander over to that bench and awkwardly set yourself upon it, making sure this causes you to have to say "Excuse me." If he looks at you, you give him a smile.

Which smile? Must it be devastatingly charming? Must it be *the smile*?

No, that is his job. Your smile can be *any* smile! I don't care if it is nervous, pale, or twitchy. If it is a smile, he will know he is allowed to interrupt your reading and speak to you. He will know he can say, "You too, huh?"

Whereupon you say, "Yeah. Another *Chicken Soup* addict. But you know what?"

He asks what, and you say, "Is chicken soup really a good thing around macramé?"

He laughs, revealing dimples. By now you have noticed that his shirt is well made and a nice easy fit, and his hair is very fingerable. He looks down at his book, and laughs again. He says, "It's even worse when it gets in your diving mask." Now his eyes are on yours, and they are very blue, and very clear, and this is when you smile at him again, and you don't say anything, you just nod.

Let's pause for a moment and say this again, because it could not be more important.

Even Mr. Right needs encouragement. If you encounter a man who looks like a good prospect to you, smile at him.

Too much smiling might make your face muscles cramp, but it also might be a sign that you have found a friend. It is amazing how quickly two people who are truly simpatico can realize that they are. Never underestimate the brilliance of the human perceptual apparatus. Don't ignore your own gut. Don't shy away from a natural, spontaneous rapport. Instead, hunker down, relax, be there. Tell yourself that *anywhere, anytime, is good for meeting Mr. Right.*

So you say, "I was just going to go next door and get a coffee. Anything but soup." You can stop there and see what he says, or if you're feeling adventurous, you can add, "Do you feel like one?" Odds are he will say yes.

And what if he says no? Well, you still did something brave, and that adds to the total amount of bravery in the universe. You suffered a small rejection, and that hurts a little, but odds are he was not unkind about it, and maybe he really had somewhere else to go.

But when it comes down to it, what have you *really* lost? The same thing men have lost down through the ages when a woman said no to *their* invite.

Nothing.

STORES IN GENERAL

My friend Anna recently explained to me that two summers ago, she went through a strange period when she must have been more attractive than usual, because men were constantly approaching her and asking her out. Anna is twenty-seven and good-looking, but often complains of not meeting any men, so the scientist in me perked up. "Were you looking different at that time?" I asked.

"No, my hair was even the same..."

"Well, where did these men mostly approach you?"

"At The Bay. I was working there for the summer before starting my new job."

"At The Bay! In what department?"
"The men's clothing department."

And there you have it. Anna thinks there was something different about her, some vibration she was exuding. If only she could recapture it...

But the truth is more basic. She was *approachable*. Men had a way of getting at her. They had a right to speak to her. They could get launched on a conversation without having to be brave, without risking a brush-off. In fact, if they walked into the right area of the store, they got approached by her.

There are two morals to this story. One concerns stores.

If you go to stores where men go, you will encounter men.

The second moral is that our old friend approachability (the second of my criteria for a good place to meet) is crucially, laughably important. Men are sighting you all the time, good men who might be just what you want. But they aren't approaching you, because they aren't comfortable making a move on someone who isn't inviting it. The only way to break this trend is to be aware of men around you, and remember that you have the option of being friendly, and of playing that card when the right time comes.

Many women have developed an almost instinctive fending-off mode that they adopt in public places. I call this "the stalker response." If they see a lone male, they avert their eyes and march on. This is useful much of the time, but it goes overboard if it discourages every man who is unlucky enough not to be already in your acquaintance from smiling at you or striking up a conversation.

Contrary to what we might think, the people on this planet whom we happen to have met are not necessarily the best people, or the most worthy candidates for friendship. Yet we tend to choose only from the people we happen to meet, no matter how happenstance the reason for meeting. Some of them become friends, and we eventually try to find a mate among them. If only there was a way to find the people we really have a lot in common with, and then meet them. (See the Internet section, Part Three.)

A man shopping has a list, and there's only one thing on it.

Back to stores. Men go to some of them. Men don't spend a lot of time browsing women's clothing (or if they do, they may not be the men you are looking for). Men don't hang out in fabric stores, or jewellery stores, or culinary stores. In fact, some would argue that men don't shop at all. They wait till they need a specific thing—say, a new frying pan for eggs—and then they rocket through the mall like a frying pan-seeking missile, not even noticing all the other stuff that they might also need or want. A man has a list, and there's only one thing on it.

Ah, you say, but guys do browse sometimes. Some men actually enjoy buying their own clothes. And men like looking at toys. Stereo equipment, computer equipment, camping equipment, sports equipment... wait, it appears that men like *equipment*.

Now, I am not suggesting that you should hang out in store aisles that don't interest you.

What I am suggesting is that you be aware of opportunities. Most women are into at least one guy thing; some are into many. So you will find yourself occasionally in a guy aisle. Be attuned to possibilities.

ART GALLERIES

There aren't that many public venues where you can be completely comfortable alone, and you can circulate freely. Where you can be totally entertained even if you have no companion. Where there is something interesting to talk about if you do have someone to talk to.

You don't need me to encourage you to go to art galleries. You just need me to tell you to be on the lookout for Mr. Right: He may be examining the Monet in the corner. That is, if he is there at all.

Which raises a burning question.

Why don't most men go to art galleries? Well of course, they do if they are in Paris with their spouse and two kids. But why don't they visit such places in their hometown?

The reason may be the same one that explains why men don't go to art films. If a woman drags a guy to an art film, he may very well enjoy it—the same for a gallery or museum. So why doesn't he go on his own? I believe the answer, which is embarrassing to the male gender, is very simple: *Men are lazy.* (I speak here of many men, not all men—some, of course, are workaholics, and some are just plain virtuous.)

Men make a much more simplistic distinction between work and play, than do women. Men hate to work, except perhaps when they are at work. They gamely make the effort to do their time each weekday at their job, in order to have an income. Then that is over and they want to avoid anything that even resembles work for the rest of the day. That means, anything that takes any effort. What they want is to play, or to wallow in immediate gratification of some sort. Now play can sometimes take a little effort: Even video machines demand some concentration, and you may have to stand up.

That is why you will find only young men in the video emporia. What is left for men of a certain age—say, over thirty? Well, two things: beer and the remote control. Beer is the maternal tit of adulthood, the soothing bosom of malt liquid. Television is the mommy across the room. Or it is the escape from that most dreaded thing: one's own life.

Single men, however, are lonely. So they don't stay at home all the time. They head out to a place where they can make no effort, receive immediate gratification, and have warm bodies around them, with whom they might even converse if pressed. That is called a bar.

An art film or an art gallery or an art anything may not have beer. It will certainly demand an effort. You have to concentrate, and reflect, and grapple, with art.

So if you do see a nice looking man smiling at you in an art venue, he already deserves a medal for having overcome the slug syndrome. Approach him with respect and optimism. Maybe he isn't gay. Maybe he is a whole lot of things that you might like.

About art gallery etiquette.

Some people are cranky about art. They don't always want to view it with someone else. To take in a great painting, these people need to have an intense personal encounter with it, a collision of universes in which their true state at that moment somehow chemically reacts with the true state of the artist at the moment they painted it. It is hard to achieve this degree of focus and vulnerability, while being diverted by someone else's thoughts.

On the other hand, many people in art galleries don't want the dizzying, terrifying, lonely rigors of such an experience.

So they walk around looking, while chatting or listening to helpful facts on headphones. And they may try to cover the whole gallery, just for completeness, whereas those who agonize over art may not be able to look at more than a handful of works in a visit.

But even the obsessive people need to rest sometimes, to turn from the painting and stroll, or settle onto a bench and digest what they have seen and felt; and moments do come when they wish they could talk to someone about it.

Such moments are gold.

FESTIVALS AND FAIRS

A bunch of happy people milling around on a sunny afternoon. Music playing, crafts for sale, grilled Polish sausage on the breeze. Women in cotton frocks, men in jeans.

What more need be said?

GYMS

Men who go to the gym have at least that in their favour. They may live longer, be more lively in bed, and be better at dragging large objects into the house.

Men at the gym can be physically inspected. So can women. Gym garb may not be all that flattering for most people, but certainly it removes the danger of nasty surprises. If a guy likes your body there, he will probably like it anywhere. And if part of your definition of Mr. Right is a lean, well-muscled specimen, the gym won't steer you wrong. The whole issue of personal appearance is disposed of in a crisp, straightforward way, so you can move on to other things. (Not that spandex is really crisp.)

On the other hand people are not always in a mood to socialize when they are sweating, trying to keep to an exercise pace, and supposed to be back at the office in twenty minutes. But there are interesting opportunities for eye contact at the gym. Often, people exercise on stationary bikes, treadmills, or other machines that keep their bodies busy, while their eyes wander...and if you're across from someone who seems to want to lock eyes with you, you can always take it from there. Wait till both of you have finished your session on the elliptical trainer. Then wander over to the water fountain in the corner. He might decide that he's thirsty too...

Then there are bars. Many, many men go to bars. Let's see if you should.

6

THE TRUTH ABOUT BARS

Why the Smart Woman Keeps an Open Mind about Them

In scores of interviews, I have heard women talk about how difficult they find it to meet good men. They list the places where they run into men but can't take advantage of it ("I meet lots of men at work, but it seems like they are always married, or clients, or gay"). Somewhere along the line they almost always say, "Of course, I don't do the bar scene anymore." Or, "I am tired of the bar scene." As if this doesn't deserve any more discussion.

But I think it does.

THE CASE AGAINST BARS: THE MEAT MARKETS

Let's admit at the start that one part of the bar scene is very obnoxious. There is a type of bar whose sole purpose seems to be casual sex. Marauding hunter-like males try to find a female victim, a prey they can "bag" before moving on to the next one on the next night. Using the sports analogy of which such men are very fond, they are out to score, and that is all they want. They are often younger men, and they are *always* immature men even if they are middle-aged, balding, and have large belt sizes.

The question is, Why do immature men want only to score?

The answer is, Who cares?

You aren't interested in immature men.

If you go to a bar that is designed to allow the immature to get sex, you are going to run into a lot of immature men.

You are looking for *mature* men, whether they are twenty-one or fifty-one (pick the age range you want). Men who are looking for a serious relationship, who want to hook up with Ms. Right. If you go to a bar that is designed to allow the immature to get sex, you are going to run into a lot of immature men. (You know the type of place: three dance floors, loud music/noise everywhere, big bouncers, no cover for ladies, free pitchers of beer on Thursday, etc. etc.) Now there may be times when you and your girlfriend just want to go dancing, or raise a little hell. Fine, head out there and burn the place up. But don't complain to me that all the guys were shallow sex-seekers, and don't claim that this proves that the "bar scene" is a waste of time.

Let us consider some other kinds of bars. But first a little proverb for you:

The best bars to meet men at, are the bars that are not for meeting men.

DESIRABLE BARS

There are three main categories of "desirable bar:" pubs, bars in good restaurants, and classy bars (these can include restaurants).

A desirable bar must have at least the following characteristics:

- It isn't too noisy to talk;
- It isn't too smoky to breathe (a vanishing problem as laws intervene);
- The seating is comfortable;
- People who are not alcoholics frequent it;
- Employed people frequent it;
- People with all their teeth frequent it;
- It serves good draft beer (or else Mr. Right may not bother with it).

This may be an astonishing notion to you, that any bar could be a desirable place to meet Mr. Right. But before we move on, open your mind for a moment and consider one man's sad experience. It has to do with pubs, my first category.

THE GLUM GANG: JACK'S STORY

Many of the men I interviewed for this book said the same thing, but none said it better than Jack. Jack is a man of forty-five, divorced, no kids. He has a few good friends who seem to have been scattered by the years. An engineer who works in city planning, he lives alone in a nice apartment where you can see photographs of his ex-wife, his brothers, and his niece in Baltimore whom he dotes on.

I ask him what he does to relax.

Jack: What do I do? I play a little golf, and some hockey in the winter. I go out for a beer.

Q: *You go out for a beer? Now, is that how you try to meet women?*

Jack: Well, it used to be. Now it's just what I do sometimes. It's been a long day, I'm tired, but I don't want to go home and sit there alone. So I go to the pub.

Q.   *And what is the pub like?*

Jack: Well, it's kind of like the one you and I are sitting in right now. [Laughs] It's comfortable, has good burgers and the blackened-salmon salad rocks. The bar itself is mahogany (as you can see), and it's extensive. A big horseshoe. I like to sit at the bar.

Q: *And what happens there?*

Jack: I smile at the nice woman bartender, I order a glass of Creemore, I hunker down on a bar stool, and I look around.

Q: *What do you see?*

Jack: I see a bunch of guys hunkered down on bar stools. [Laughs]

Q: *You really seem to have this method nailed. Does it bring you big results?*

Jack: Man, I am serious. I have seen the same thing my whole life. A bunch of lonely guys, and no women. It is pathetic.

Q: *You never see any women?*

Jack: Sure. I'll see a girl with some guy: He's showing off because he has one.

Q: *Right. [Laughs]*

Jack: Right. The only reason he brought her there was to show her off to the Gallery. The dudes at the bar. So we all steal glances at her, and we think, "Yeah, that's one of them females, all right!"

Q: *Jack, I have to ask you in all seriousness, because this is what I am researching, are you saying that you do or don't go there to meet women?*

Jack: Hell, I don't go there thinking I will meet a woman. But I guess in the back of my mind, there might be a woman there. I might at least see a woman. [laughs]

Q: *That sounds like a good bet.*

Jack: Yeah, I see women with a man. Or I see women in a group.

Q: *Do you approach them?*

Jack: The women? Hell no. What do you think I am, brave?

Q: *I guess not. [laughs]*

Jack: Do I want to stand there while two girlfriends watch the third girlfriend reject me? I've never been pushy.

Q: *So, not a good track record.*

Jack: Okay, one time a lady sat down beside me on a Saturday night. I couldn't believe it. A nice-looking brunette.

Q: *What happened?*

Jack: I started talking to her, she was friendly, I liked her. An intelligent woman, just wanted a drink. We talked for like, two hours.

Q: *Did you ask her out?*

Jack: I didn't. I'm nuts. I thought it might spoil things. I wasn't getting that signal from her. Once we started talking, she told me about her separation from her husband. They were still not sure where it was going. I liked her though.

Q: *So, other than that...*

Jack: Nothing. Nada. Just a bunch of men. The Glum Gang.

The moral of the story: You don't know Jack.

The terrible truth, which women have been urged not to believe, is this: **Bars are crawling with Mr. Rights—just crawling with them**.

Remember that I am not talking about undesirable, meat-market bars. For the rest of this chapter, I am talking about bars where perfectly okay men go. Why do they go there? To avoid total loneliness, which is waiting for them at home.

Suppose for a moment that the world changed completely one day, in a sort of *Twilight Zone* transformation, and Jack wandered into a bar and found what he had never found before. Women had shown up, alone. Not just one woman, but lots of women.

JACK'S GOOD DREAM:
THE DAY THE WORLD MADE SENSE

Jack arrives at his watering hole at 6:30 p.m., feeling bedraggled and put upon. He has trouble finding a place at the bar; the place seems more crowded than usual, and slightly abuzz. But he spots a vacant stool on the far side and sits down, wondering what is wrong. He glances to left and right, and he sees a woman on each side of him! Jack's heart begins to pit-pat, and his palms break into a sweat! Feminism has offered up unexpected fruits—equality is afoot!

Jack orders a draft, a large, and hazards a longer look around. There are eligible women everywhere—he counts eight of them on first survey; there are maybe seven men in the bar area. He glances at the woman on his left. She has shoulder-length brown hair, and is wearing a shirt in a cool shade of blue. She smiles at him.

"This can't be happening," Jack thinks. "This does not happen. *Women don't go to bars alone.*"

But even in dreams one must try. Alice said that in Wonderland. Jack ends up talking to three different women before he is done.

Jack wonders what is wrong: there's a woman on each side of him!

After an hour or so he realizes who it is, in the whole room, he most wants to be talking to. It is a green-eyed girl who is two seats over: She has short auburn hair and a warm, feisty smile, and he has overheard her talking about movies with the woman on his right. She hated *Titanic*, as did Jack; and she hated *Terminator II*, but she loved the original *Terminator*. Jack finds this too endearing for words. He is a bit of a film nut and he never finds people who share his passion, let alone (some of) his opinions.

Without thinking, Jack rises up from his stool and walks over to this woman. "What bothered you about *Terminator II?*" he says.

"They betrayed their whole concept, about evil machines, just because Arnold wanted to be warm and fuzzy," she says, with a challenge in her eyes. Jack stands there grinning.

"Do you find something amusing?" she says.

"No," Jack says. "God no." And they begin to talk.

Two hours later they are still talking. About the movie they are going to see Thursday night, at the new upscale Cineplex that even shows a few art movies.

…And they would talk forever, if Jack didn't hear the jangle of his clock radio, and reluctantly wake up to the real world. Where women don't go to bars alone.

WHY WOMEN DON'T GO TO BARS ALONE

Six Myths *Not* to Live By

*W*hile I was working on this book I took an informal survey, asking women the deceptively innocent question, "Would you go to a bar alone?" In most cases I was met with a kind of playful shock and outrage. I felt as if I had stumbled onto a piece of cultural—or biological—bedrock.

"No!" they said.

"Of course not!"

"Are you crazy?"

Isn't this interesting, I thought. Could this be a real difference between the genders? I couldn't even *ask* a man this question. He wouldn't understand what I was getting at. He would say, "What do you mean—why *wouldn't* I go to a bar alone?"

So I asked the women why not. I guess I was expecting safety to be the main answer, and I'd been thinking about that myself (see Myth 6 below). But safety turned out not to be the leader—not even close. Other reasons came pouring out, interesting reasons. Before long they started to be repeated when

I asked new women, and I knew my basic list was close to complete.

The reasons I was given turned out to be colourful and magnetic, but in the end every one could be refuted. That is why I will present them as six myths.

Walking through the doors of a pub doesn't suddenly turn a man into a feral animal.

There was one other point: Something struck me as familiar about these myths. Then I realized that I had heard them before, when women were giving me their reasons for not seeking a partner on the Internet, for not wanting to put a profile and photo online. The very same reasons that keep some women away from the number one real-world situation where men can be easily met, also keep them away from the leading *virtual* location where men can be met. That is why these myths are doubly important, and why we must confront them, now and in Part Three of this book.

If my survey was right, you will probably be able to guess many of...

THE SIX MYTHS THAT DISCOURAGE WOMEN FROM GOING TO A BAR ALONE

MYTH NO. 1: Men in bars only want one thing.

This is utter hogwash.

Of course, men in meat-market bars are often looking to score.

But for the average guy in what we have called a desirable bar, a one-night stand is the last thing on his mind. He is like our friend Jack. He wants a drink and maybe someone to make a little conversation with. He wants to relax. If the totally improbable happens and a nice woman sits down beside him, the last thing he wants to do is blow this unheard-of chance by coming on too strong.

Men are aware of the dislike women have for pushy, overly aggressive, cliché-spewing come-on artists!

And men don't like rejection, any more than you do. It's humiliating.

The farthest the average guy is going to go in a desirable bar, if he feels that he has hit it off with you, is maybe to try to find a way to contact you in the future. He may try to get your phone number. Or he may try to give you his. If you don't want to give this information, you don't have to.

The men in desirable bars are a cross section of the male population. They want the same things that they would want if they weren't in a bar. High on this list: someone nice to go out with. This is not a bad thing; this is a good thing. Walking through the doors of a pub doesn't suddenly turn a man into a feral animal.

And walking through the doors of a pub doesn't stop Mr. Right from being Mr. Right. It just makes him easy for you to access.

MYTH NO. 2: Only sluts go to bars alone.
or, If I go alone, they'll think I'm a slut.

It is hard to believe that at the start of the twenty-first century, women could still be browbeaten by a sexist dilemma from the 1950s, but according to the interviews I have done, they are. The problem goes all the way back to a time when the nice girl/slut distinction was cast in stone. A "nice girl" was one who hung on to her virginity until marriage, or close to it, and who would not "put out" or "go all the way." A "slut" was a girl who would "give her body" to at least some askers. *But the essence of the slut was that she admitted that she wanted sex.* It was okay to want it, as long as you didn't admit this fact.

Then came the sexual revolution of the sixties; then came progress for women on a variety of fronts; then came HIV. And today we live in a world where adult un-attached women are much more comfortable with their sexuality, and where the big issue about sex is not, "Are you having it?" but "Are you liking it?" and "Are you having it safely?" and "Is it leading anywhere?"

Yet the fifties still cling. Why can't the typical woman feel comfortable walking into a bar alone? Because she thinks that amounts to asking for sex—which brands her as a slut. She may not think this consciously: she knows that "slut" was a term invented to oppress females, and that it implies a double standard in which men who want sex are smiled on, women condemned. But all this doesn't help her walk into the bar. She is still affected by shadowy stereotypes from the past.

Ah, you say, but what about men? Women won't be free of these stereotypes until men are too. That's a good point; there probably are some men who still are influenced by the same nasty dogma. But many men, I would argue, are not. So men and women both, let's dispel the myth and stand on the truth.

The truth is that you need no more reason than a man to walk into a bar alone. You feel like a drink. You feel like chatting with somebody. You want to unwind, but don't feel like being at home. And if you choose a desirable bar, and conduct yourself with your usual dignity, no one will assume that you are some raving nymphomaniac on the loose. No one will question you about your motivation. In fact, you may find yourself ignored, unless you give a friendly cue to someone. On the other hand, you are alone, so if you want to be approached, you will very likely have no trouble bringing this about.

The truth is that a woman alone in a respectable bar is in a position of total advantage.

MYTH NO. 3: A woman cannot call the shots in a bar; it is a male stronghold.

Not to repeat myself, but no one has power like a woman in a desirable bar.

Are you afraid of that power? Don't be, it is too valuable. Wield it like the warrior goddess you are. Know that you hold the best cards, and treat the whole experience as a jolly adventure, an amusing experiment in human relations.

You may feel that you are a sitting duck in a shooting gallery. You may think that you can only talk to the guys who talk to you, that the men, by their actions or inaction, run the show. You can't sit everywhere; what if you choose a bad stool and the guy next to you is a dud? Trip wasted?

You have a right under the Constitution to get up from your seat, sidle over, and say, "Do you like the draft here?"

Not at all. What you have to do is establish your own territory, study your drink rather carefully, relax, and begin to perceive what is around you. Stop being the "look-ee" and become the "look-er." Guys do this all the time. If you are a businesswoman, you have probably learned long ago to do this in conference rooms, at sales meetings, etc. Do the same thing in a desirable bar, and do it alone. Look at a few guys, inspect them like Patton inspecting his troops. Do it with casual disinterest, impartiality, unconcern. Not in an unfriendly way, just observant. Watch them look away.

How do you fend off the guy who approaches (or is already next to you), and is a talker and a waste of time? You give him two minutes of civil chatter, then you say firmly and without tension, "I need to look at something here, can you excuse me?" And you produce a document from your purse. Or you say, "I need a minute to recharge here, okay?" Then take away your attention. Whatever, just be firm and civil. Most guys will quickly back off. They aren't drunk; they aren't stupid. Desirable bars don't tolerate stupid drunks.

Inspect some guys. Watch them, listen to them. (People watching is fun!) See how they interact, who looks blue, who looks bored. Who looks good. Who would you like to talk to if it were possible. If you find anyone worthy, there are two questions.

One: Does he think the same about you?

Two: If he does, how do you make something happen?

Now you have to accept that maybe he won't find you attractive. If not, that's okay, nothing lost. (That will just make him a failed candidate; and your job is to eliminate lots of them on the way to Mr. Right.) But at the start, go ahead and assume he will react positively, and let your gaze fall upon him, and smile.

You will know from his reaction whether he is interested; it will be all too clear. If he is, he will smile back, maybe look away, but keep looking back... And he will want to approach you, and chances are he will do so. If he doesn't stir from his seat, but is obviously interested, guess what? You have a right under the Constitution to get up from your seat, sidle over, and say, "Do you like the draft here?" or any other lame ice-breaker that you can think of. Men have been doing this for hundreds of years—try it and see how it makes you feel. Chances are you won't find out how it makes a typical guy feel, because your initiative will be so surprising and welcome, even shocking, that no matter how lame your entrée, it will get you in.

A WOMAN DECIDES TO DO A LITTLE SASHAYING HERSELF

While I was working on this book, I sent a partial draft of it to a female friend (let's call her Kathy), including the section on bars.

The same week she read it, Kathy happened to be meeting her sister in San Francisco. It was a Saturday afternoon, they were going to shop and hang out, they had agreed to start with a quick drink at a cool bar in North Beach. Kathy got there first. Normally she would wait for her sister by the doorway; but she had been reading my book. She couldn't resist a try-out. She walked in and sat at the end of the L-shaped bar, ordered a martini and struck up a witty conversation with the bartender. Soon two men who had sat down nearby began to tune in on her. One of them, who was right next to her across the corner of the L, began to talk to Kathy.

Kathy made several observations. The other guy, who wasn't talking, was very attractive but seemed shy and a bit aloof. Then she noticed something else. "I never would have caught it if I hadn't just read your book," she e-mailed me. "The second guy, the quiet one, was every now and then stealing a glance at me, and as soon as I looked at him, he would look away. I immediately thought, *He's having a sighting*!

"So I did two crazy things that I would never do. First, I waited for him to look again, and when he did, I gave him a big, fearless smile—caught him by surprise. He smiled back and actually turned a little red. His friend got up to go to the bathroom, and *then I really broke with tradition.* I got up from my stool, walked over, and sat down on the empty stool on the far side of Mr. Sighting. I actually turned towards him, so my knees were pulled up in front of him, and I started chatting with him."

Kathy was dressed to the nines that day—feeling good about herself. She is not conventionally beautiful, but she is definitely attractive and her hazel eyes are amazing. Unfortunately she suffers from shaky self-esteem, and on some days she is convinced that no sane man would want her. On other days, and usually when her sister is in the mix, she becomes zanier and throws her self-criticisms to the wind.

And on this day, she was astute enough to notice that this particular guy definitely was ogling her. So she talked to him. And it turned out he was intelligent, funny, and had a creative job (in Web design). "It was so great," she told me. "I didn't feel put upon or under the microscope, because I was the one who had sashayed over to him. I felt confident." By the time Kathy's sister got there, in the natural course of the conversation they had learned about each other's jobs and exchanged cards.... It was that easy.

Since then they have started dating, and things are promising.

MYTH NO. 4: A woman who goes to a bar alone looks like she is *desperate* for love.

This unworthy doctrine is destructive the way only a *self-inflicted double standard* can be. Men constantly go to bars alone. Nobody—not other men, not women—charges them with desperation. Nobody says, "Oh, he wants a beer; he must be desperate for love." Yet many women seriously believe that if they walk into a desirable bar and quench their thirst, they might as well be wearing a sign that reads, "I'm so-oooo lonely. Please love me!"

Why would anyone think this? Well, there is one reason that could be floated, I suppose. The argument would go like this: Such behaviour is unusual. In other words, it is unusual to see a woman walk alone into a bar and sit down and order a drink. What would drive a woman to do something so unusual? It must be loneliness. She is love-starved.

This is a silly argument. It strains like crazy to find a far-fetched answer, when easy explanations are nearby. Maybe she is thirsty. Maybe she wants to kick back for a few minutes before hitting the traffic. Maybe she is waiting for someone, got here early and feels like a drink. Maybe she is a sociable person with an hour to kill. Maybe the movie doesn't start for a while. Maybe she knows the bartender. Maybe she owns the damn place. Whatever. She has a right to walk in and take up space.

Consider. If *two* women walk into a bar, does everyone whisper behind their hands, "OH, OH! Love-starved!" Of course not. So what's the difference? Are we to believe that women are so dependent on being with someone else that the only reason they would appear in public, without an ally to cling to, must be abject desperation? Why can't we envision a self-reliant woman who just happens to be alone in public? The answer is, we can. *Men can.*

I return to this theme of not going out alone in later chapters. It is a crucial building block, indeed perhaps the cornerstone, of the prison that prevents women from meeting the worthy men who are all around them.

MYTH NO. 5: Serious relationships never begin in bars.
It was a winter night, 11 p.m. My car wouldn't start, in a parking lot way downtown. I knew it was the mysterious "water thing" that my Ford does to me at least once a year. Condensation somewhere inside the engine renders it immobile; mechanics can find nothing wrong; the next day it runs fine.

Nothing to do but call the tow service, so I did. The truck pulled up a half hour later, the man hooked my car up, I climbed in his cab, and we hit the highway for home.

His name was Frank. Frank was a salt of the earth type guy, friendly, talkative. He had one peculiarity: He kept sticking his head out the window, like some hound dog. It was cold and I didn't appreciate the gale coming into the truck. He must have known what I was thinking, and he explained over the roar of the engine and the wind that he had claustrophobia, had it bad, and even sitting in the cab of the truck was hard to do. The only relief was to stick his head out the window—I guess it was his way of bonding with a larger space.

I took a liking to this rough-hewn, open, vulnerable character who had just rescued me from a cold fate. I asked him a few questions, it didn't take much effort on my part, soon he was telling me about his wonderful wife. "She is smart, works with computers, programs them. Makes good money." It seems that Frank and his wife had been unable to have kids, so they started adopting. They had adopted three children—two of them were to avoid separating brother from sister, one was disabled—when one of their own came along. So now they have four. As he yelled out his life story to me over the noise from his open window, I could tell that Frank was a loving, hard-working man with a huge heart and a good marriage. A lucky man who had found real happiness in giving, and who had lucked into a superb woman whom he worshipped.

I couldn't resist asking, "Frank, how did you meet your wife?"

He told me that one night some friends threw a bachelor party for a guy. Frank went—a pal gave him a ride. It was at a quaint old bar north of town, the kind where people dance to a little band. Frank got bored with the group he was with, the drinking, the phony rituals with a hired stripper. Frank wandered over to another section of the bar. Two women were talking at a table. One of them looked awful good to Frank. Frank never approaches women he doesn't know, hardly ever goes to bars. The other woman got up and went to the phone booth. Frank spoke to the one he liked. He ended up talking to her and her friend for two hours. "She thought she knew what I wanted," Frank told me. "I told her I wasn't like that, I just would like to call her. She said she never went to bars, her girl-friend had dragged her out tonight. I said I was the same. She didn't believe me. But she finally gave me her number."

That was it. Frank found Ms. Right. Frank hit the jackpot. If not for that reluctant trip to a bar that two people made that night, maybe Frank is still alone. Maybe that big heart of his goes to waste. And now, four kids later, Frank's story spills a little warmth my way, as we ride the streets towards home.

MYTH NO. 6: A woman is not safe in a bar alone.

We've touched on issues of psychological comfort and safety above (see myths one to four). We're talking here about *physical safety*, a different and valid concern. I'm not suggesting that you go to a bar alone unless you not only *are* safe, but you feel safe, too. It just wouldn't be much fun.

Now obviously we're not talking here about a bar where the reddish gloom smells like violence and the mood leans towards crazy and out-of-control. I wouldn't feel safe there either, unless I was with my songwriter friend who is a former boxer with an easy stance that discourages all comers.

No, we're talking about a desirable bar. It is friendly, nicely lit, not overly rowdy, and the patrons are decent human beings. You've been there before and feel comfortable in the place. The bartender is easy to talk to (and gorgeous). You know some of the regulars, and if you needed someone's help, they would gladly give it.

Or maybe you've got a place in mind that you're not so familiar with. You could check it out with a friend, get to know the bartender or a waitress.

In other words, structure the situation to where you feel safe. If that means going to an upscale restaurant bar an hour before your friend meets you there for dinner, and using valet parking, so be it. Or if it means going to a pub where the proprietor wants to adopt you, that's fine too.

Which doesn't mean you shouldn't take standard precautions, en route and inside the premises. Use the same safety measures as you would going to any public place alone. Carry your cell phone and make sure it's fully charged. Have 911 on speed dial. If you drive, go to a place with accessible, well-lit parking, or use valet parking. When you get in your car, don't sit there talking on your cell; turn the key and hit the road. Carry cash for a taxi, and if anything feels wrong when you're returning to your car, go back inside and call a cab.

Better safe than sorry. But better visible than invisible.

A BONUS NOTE ON PUBS

A pub is a place where ordinary people gather to sip drinks and talk, or think, or stare at the game on a silent TV, or play a little darts. In Britain (and Chicago) every neighbourhood, every street corner, has one. A pub isn't pretentious, isn't fancy. No one cares what you wear. Business people can wander in and be at home; so can bohemian poets. There is good draft beer, preferably from local microbreweries. The food is cheap and flavourful. There are some good wines open. There tend to be regulars, but no one cares if you are a regular or not. The atmosphere is not as fishbowl-like as the bar on *Cheers*, where everyone knows your name and whole soap operas are enacted for their amusement.

In North America some cities have real British-style pubs, and others don't, but I define the term very broadly, to include your average slightly rumpled, friendly bar, where people go mostly to socialize: as long as there is not loud music, or sports events with sound turned on—in a word, there can't be loud anything, unless it's people's voices...

A pub is a little bit like a private party, in that you can feel free to speak to a stranger without seeming out of line. Especially if you are a woman. A man may be a bit leery of speaking to a woman he doesn't know, because she may think he is coming on to her, or otherwise invading her personal space; but a woman who speaks to a man is very unlikely to receive a rebuff.

It's a mild evening. A good man who would love to meet you is quite possibly sitting in a pub right now. There's an empty stool beside him.

8

GOING OUT ALONE

Warning: This Could Lead to Fabulous Encounters!

$\mathcal{T}$hink of two women, chatting animatedly in a restaurant bar, leaning over the table to bond with each other, bonding about the difficulty of meeting eligible men. Then consider the fact that by being there together, by relying on the comfort of another's company, they are creating the very situation that seems to be driving them nuts.

Okay, hanging with friends is excellent fun, and something we all love to do. But when it comes to your quest for Mr. Right, it sometimes needs to take a back seat. Being an intrepid loner has its pleasures too. It is exciting and highly entertaining—even if it may sometimes feel a little silly or lonely. But if you want to meet a man, you have to pay a price. You have to take a risk or two.

Let's reverse the tables, literally, and see how it feels. Imagine that you have taken our previous chapter to heart, and are out in a desirable bar alone, wearing something cool. After surveying the patrons for a while, you notice a guy in a green shirt who looks like your type. He's attractive, seems comfortable in his own skin, and has an intelligent air. Suddenly, you realize what's going on: You are having a *sighting*. The only problem is, he's at a table with two other guys and the three of them are doing what people sometimes do in bars, hooting and hollering. You like your green-shirted guy, but you aren't so sure about the other two, and you notice that one of them, the tall red-haired one, spends a lot of time sizing up women in a crude way and then commenting on them to the third guy, a stocky fellow with glasses.

So you find it hard to approach them. You are safe at your own table but if you go over to them you'll feel like a deer in the headlights.

You keep thinking, "If only he was alone." Even then it would take courage to just walk up to him and start a conversation, but at least you wouldn't have the whole class staring at you while you did it! Did I say the whole class? If you've ever had an awkward stage—say, in high school—it feels like you're channelling that past self, right now.

Now reverse the situation and you will know how hard it is for an average guy to approach you when you are camped with other women at a table.

You keep thinking, "If only he was alone." Mr. Right may be sitting across the room, observing you, appreciating you, and desiring you. But like Jack in our interview, he doesn't want to stand before the mocking tribunal of your girlfriends. (It's like submitting work to a committee: Someone in the group is bound to dislike it.) He wants to level the playing field, he wants to talk to you one-on-one.

You may very well have gone out tonight at least partially with the idea of meeting men. But for comfort's sake, you have sabotaged your own goal. Go ahead and sit there, enjoy the merriment of your girlfriends, but know this: You may be quarantining yourself from the very man you want to meet.

Now I know there is a type of man who is cocky enough to approach a bunch of women and perform for them, complacent in the belief that every one will be conquered by his charm and good looks. Men like this may be diverting, but they tend to be arrogant, shallow, and a bad bet for a relationship.

Do you have any reason to believe that Mr. Right is cocky in that way?

If, after thinking about what I've said in this and the preceding chapter, you still can't bring yourself to sit in a desirable bar alone, then go ahead and take a girlfriend with you. But consider the following rule of thumb, which applies equally to women and men:

The one who isn't alone should approach the one who is.

The one who isn't alone has moral support. Companions to egg her on. Allies to comfort her if her mission fails. So she should make the move, take the risk. (Or he should, if the guy is with friends and the woman is alone.)

Is that so unfair? If you are with your girlfriends and you notice a guy who is alone, and you like his style, and he seems to be noticing you, then you should get up from your table and go over to him and say hello.

Or at the very least, give him an unmistakable clue that his approach would be welcome. Give him a good smile; buy him a drink; do *something* to rouse his bravery.

THE FRIEND WHO DIDN'T LET A SIGHTING GO TO WASTE

Karen was an animal trainer in Ottawa. She was also a very

beautiful woman, admired and loved by her clients, or should we say her clients' owners. She was willowy, blonde, and had unearthly blue eyes that made you feel you were in the presence of an angel, or a visitor from a superior planet.

Unfortunately she lived a modest life socially. She worked so hard that there wasn't time to go out at night. She wasn't really comfortable in bars. Most of the guys she met were dogs—or horses.

But once upon a time, she received an invitation, a funny card signed by a dog named Budge. It was really from Budge's owners, who wanted Karen to attend a party at a famous music venue, where a friend's independent CD was being released.

"He is your exact type. He obviously likes you. You have to talk to him." The invitation was too cute to resist, so Karen talked her friend Amy into going with her, and they showed up at the club and sat at the bar. Budge's owners, who had never seen Karen outside her office, hardly recognized her, but when they did, they greeted her with joyous hugs.

The music was great, Karen and Amy had a good time, and when it was over they didn't feel like calling it a night. After all, they might not do this again for years.

So they went to another nightspot, this one a fine restaurant, and they sat down at the bar and ordered martinis.

After a while Amy noticed a guy sitting down at the other end of the bar. He seemed to be staring at Karen. He didn't get up to talk to them, he just sat there sipping his drink and looking long and often at Karen.

Amy said, "He is your exact type. He obviously likes you. You have to talk to him."

Amy said this many times. Amy cajoled and argued, joked and pleaded.

Karen said "No no no, what are you thinking, me approach a strange guy in a bar? Are you out of your mind?"

Amy said, "You may never see him again. Look at the way he's looking at you. This is a special moment. You have to talk to him." (If she had read this book, she would have said, "He is having a *sighting*, silly.")

After about an hour of this, Karen did an amazing thing. She got up, walked around the bar, and sat down with the guy (Peter was his name).

They started talking. And talking. And talking. It turned out that he was a little depressed because he had been to the funeral of a dear friend that day. But he was glad of the company.

Amy watched them. Karen waved to her and smiled at her and she kept talking to Peter for three hours. Karen had been seeing someone for over a year, but by the ten-minute mark of her conversation with Peter, she was wondering what she had been thinking with that other guy.

Six months later Karen and Peter were married.

So here are two axioms, the second revisited for good measure:

The brave woman does not let a sighting go to waste.
and
The one who isn't alone should approach the one who is.

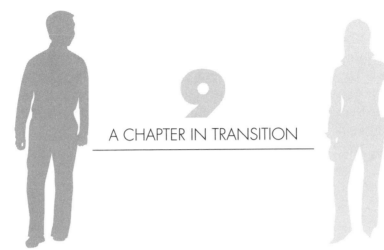

9

A CHAPTER IN TRANSITION

*R*eader, we have come pretty far.

We have seen how you can take charge of your own destiny, and set sail like a buccaneer onto the glinting seas where Mr. Right is looking for you.

Those seas will take us to another land before long, a fertile land that we need to explore: the world of online mating. That is Part Three of our journey. I will provide you with the best map and compass that my research and experience can offer, and you will find that if you are really serious about finding a lifetime partner, the Internet is the answer to your prayers.

But before we go there, we need to tackle another area.

We need to discuss the trickiest issue of all: When these methods bring you face to face with a good prospect, how do you tell whether he is really right for you? You will be faced with a good number of promising men. So like the senate when the president proposes a new candidate for the Supreme Court, you'll have to vet them.

With the help of gripping vignettes and incisive explanations, we'll tease out what compatibility means for you in a number of areas such as baggage, trust, personality, sex, life goals, politics, and religion. These insights will help you outwit the attractions of Mr. Wrong, and recognize the merits of Mr. Right when he comes face to face with you.

That is Part Two, and it starts now.

PART

RECOGNIZING MR. RIGHT

The True and False
Signs of Compatibility

10

COMPATIBILITY 101

Baggage, Sex, Love, and Trust

$\mathcal{A}$ library's worth of words has been written on the subject of how to find a good man. "Look out for the bad man," they tell you. "You don't want him!" Experts trumpet the recipe for a good man, the signs of a bad one.... They teach you to steer away from men who are distant, angry, men with baggage, men who can't love, men who use women, men who are commitment-phobic.

These discussions all miss the boat. They all share a crucial, simple-minded assumption that is, unfortunately, wrong.

They all assume that men are either good or bad, intrinsically. That every man is one or the other. But the truth is, a man may be bad for Cindy but good for Paula. Any man in the wrong relationship is likely to behave badly. (So is any woman.)

So much pain, so many tears could be avoided, if women followed this advice:

Don't look for a good man. Look for a man who is good *for you.*

Now it is a fact: Some men are of better character than others. Some men are criminals. Some are sadists. Some are cheaters and liars and thieves and philanderers. But this doesn't help us. We already knew that. Mom told us to avoid those kinda guys. *Of course* you should avoid men of bad character.

But expecting perfection is a whole other bag. Only perfect people should seek it.

Are you perfect for *every* man? Could you be dropped into *any* relationship and still do fine—even if you had nothing in common with the guy? Have you always treated well every man that you have been involved with?

Ever dumped anybody? Ever rejected anybody? Ever been accused of leading anyone on? Of being cruel? Of being bossy? Of being cold? Of being bored? Ever had someone be very attracted to you, but you weren't attracted back?

Sure you have. We all have. If you haven't, you're a saint, and you need to read those self-help books that imply that their readers are all innocent and nice and would never hurt a fly, and if anything bad happens to them it's some man's fault.

This book is for women who realize that they could be good partners for some men, but not for all. And who are fair-minded enough to understand that a given man out there may be a bad partner for one woman, but he may be very good for some other.

So what is it we should be looking for?

What we want is compatibility. If you hook up with the right person for you, nature will make sure that the kinks get worked out. There will be so much sap in the tree, so much gas in the tank, so much good will and passion and respect on both sides, so much positive experience from day to day, so many little moments in which you feel that "Wow, this person is awesome, I am enjoying this," and so much ability to communicate with each other when things are happy that when they get snarled up, problems will be overcome. The demons each of you carry into the relationship will fight a losing battle against the love you bear each other.

THE TRUTH ABOUT BAGGAGE

For we all have demons. We have not lived our lives in Eden (and even there, I hear, there was trouble).

That is why it is so ridiculous when the mating-and-dating books tell you, "Beware baggage!" Read the personal ads and you will find women following this rule, announcing that the man they seek must have no baggage. He has to be financially secure, tall, honest, and have no baggage.

What a crock.

Everyone has baggage. Everyone is affected by past problems with family or friends or lovers, and by bad experiences from the past, whether at school, work, or play. If someone claims to be totally unscathed, they are living in la-la land.

The question is not whether a person has baggage, but how a person handles their baggage, and whether they *can* handle it.

Any man in the wrong relationship is likely to behave badly. (So is any woman.)

When two people who are right for each other get together, what is the first thing that they do, once they settle down to serious talk? They open up their psychic suitcases, and they compare baggage. They talk about their pasts, they air out their griefs, guilts, doubts, and fears. They lovingly, earnestly share these things with each other, hoping against hope that this person can be entrusted with this fragile freight. That finally, they may have met someone who can understand where they have been, and help them journey on to a new place.

How the other person processes the story of your journey so far, is a major indicator of whether he is any good for you.

Does he really listen? Does he get it? Does he empathize? Do the two of you start to laugh at how sick life can be sometimes? (Humour will be the great healer for you two, if you are right for each other.) Do you see each other's past loves, not as competition or as threatening, but as assets (however bittersweet) that brought you to where your paths could meet? Does he find material in his own past that chimes with what you have been through? Does he love you for your mistakes? Do you love him for being the battered, bruised, yet unbowed boxer that he is?

Do you like the way he assesses his own baggage? Does he seem honest, contrite, self-critical? Then maybe you've got something there.

Baggage is not bad. Baggage is the burden of a human soul.

Unless it's too heavy to carry...

He isn't carrying his baggage, he's lying underneath it.

If a man seems to be crippled by his baggage, that ain't good. If he is obsessed, if all he can talk about is his cruel or evil ex, his poor unfortunate ex, or worst of all, his beautiful unattainable ex, that's all you need to know. He is trapped in the past. He isn't carrying his baggage, he's lying underneath it.

Beware also the man who can't even open his baggage, who must keep it under lock and key or deny that it's even there. If you try to ask him what happened in such-and-such a situation, or what went wrong with so-and-so, he slams a steel door in your face and makes you understand that you must never go there. Such a man probably has festering sore spots, violent emotions of hurt and rage clustered around disasters from his past. He is in denial as to his own issues and must make you a co-conspirator in his cover-up. He may encourage you to air out your own baggage, but any data you give him is likely to be misused.

So look for a man who is comfortable with his own baggage, and with yours. And celebrate the wisdom that experience brings.

Which brings up an interesting point: People sometimes learn from their failures.

THE PAST IS NOT ALWAYS A PICTURE OF THE FUTURE, AND OTHER REFLECTIONS

People learn. They make adjustments, they try a different tack. Their previous relationship may be a good guide to their next one, exactly because the next one is the exact opposite of the last. (I'm not saying this happens always, or even most of the time. I'm saying it happens often enough to be worth considering.)

Sometimes you will hear a woman complain, "If only he had been that way with *me* [the way he is with his new squeeze], we would have worked out fine." It seems that the lessons she tried to teach him suddenly sank in, once he was with his new lover.

These kinds of things happen all the time:

- A man who is the poster boy for commitment-phobia, leaves the woman he has been stringing along for fifteen years and marries his next girlfriend in six months.
- A man who was always fighting and threatening to break up with Rhonda, moves in with Wendy and becomes a peaceful lion.

What causes these pesky turn-arounds, these 180s?

Well, maybe it's hard to give someone what she wants if a guy feels like that would make him the loser in the ongoing war the two are having. But nevertheless his heart hears her complaints, sees her suffer, and files the lesson away for his next relationship.

Or maybe the new person is chosen specifically for having the qualities that were lacking in the old one. People aren't dumb: They notice what is annoying them and sabotaging them. So they go out and find someone who isn't like that. And that enables *them* to behave in a different way.

When your needs are being met, you become a nicer person. Men do, too.

So a guy's track record is not always a perfect guide to what he may be capable of. Again, he may have been bad for Jill, but he may be perfect for Lil.

Here's a revealing experiment: *Ask him what his ex would say about him.*

Can he answer this? (And can you? It isn't so easy.)

Try him. If he laughs sheepishly and spills some fairly awful stuff that she would say, and says "She's probably right," then he may be the kind of honest, contrite, self-critical fellow who can actually learn from his mistakes, one who can take the blame when it belongs to him. In short, a fair-minded person. If he is reluctant to trash her, yet is clear on how they didn't click together, this too may be good. If, on the other hand, he always finds that someone else was to blame for whatever went wrong, look out.

Just to sum up so far, don't look for a perfect man. Look for a man who is compatible with you. Which brings us to the million-dollar question: How do you tell if a man is compatible with you?

This is the hardest question. This is the toughest challenge, the snare that lies behind most failed relationships. The issue people don't pay attention to, the pitfall they ignore at their peril.

What makes it especially difficult is that other things can so easily masquerade as compatibility.

In the next chapters we will look at the areas where compatibility can be found. But first, let's look at three of the false signs along the road.

We would all agree that sex and love matter—right? Yes they do, but the trouble is, they matter too much. They are at the top of the list of...

THINGS THAT CAN BE MISTAKEN FOR COMPATIBILITY

1. Sexual Attraction: Signpost to Heaven, or Gateway to Hell?

The trouble with sexual attraction is, couples have to have it to succeed, but it is so not enough. And unfortunately, at its most powerful it does a good job of seeming to be enough!

Look at couples who are totally miserable and ask yourself, "What on earth possessed them to think they could get along?" You have to answer in most cases: they had a sexual attraction. Back at the beginning, they looked at each other and they lusted. Oh, the chemistry. The spell it cast. It seemed to fill the universe, it made them forget about all other needs. Or even more diabolically, it made the other areas seem as if they were clicking perfectly. Caught up in the dance of desire, the two of them *seemed* so good together. Did they talk cleverly? Yes! Did they laugh uproariously? Yes! Did they enjoy any kind of outing, never ceasing to be entertained? Yes yes yes.

But look at them now. Two years later. They don't talk much. They don't laugh. They avoid being alone together. It's easier for him to be with the TV than with her. And worst of all, they hardly ever have sex, and when they do, it isn't very good.

That is what happens when people choose each other based on sexual attraction *alone*.

Now why would people do that?

Guys go and stand like John Cusack in the rain and hold up a boom box and play some romantic anthem.

Sad to say, many people don't have any idea that they should look for anything more than sexual attraction. They don't even have the *concept* of compatibility. It doesn't occur to them that a husband and wife should be real friends; maybe they never saw this in their own parents. Maybe they don't expect it from the opposite gender. They've grown up thinking friends are the people you don't have sex with.

And although (or because) we live in a culture obsessed with sex, many people don't feel all that attractive, and are pretty happy when mutual chemistry happens. So they jump at it.

It's no surprise that many women have a very strong agenda of having babies. This agenda often gets delayed these days, and when it kicks in with a vengeance in the mid-to-late thirties or even later, several things have happened. She has gotten older. Maybe she doesn't weigh 115 pounds any more. Bombarded by endless sexy images of thin twenty-year-olds, maybe she doesn't really feel that she can compete. Worst of all, she is past the years when it was easy to meet men, when it happened without really trying.

Then somehow, he comes along, a guy who seems to want her, who isn't married or gay or a nutcase. He still has his teeth, can put words together into sentences, and his member performs when she wants it to. So she takes the plunge. She bets on this horse. Not willing to wait any longer, not willing to take a chance on letting this one slip away, she goes for it.

Oh, and boy, is she good at ignoring the red flags that anyone else would see. So he complains a lot about how everyone else mistreats him. So he is vague about his financial affairs. So his friends drink a lot. So he speaks ill of his ex-wife. So what? He's viable, he wants the job. He even showed up with flowers once.

And they're having sex. And the sex isn't bad. So this will work, right? Wrong.

Oh, and one other thing. Sexual attraction so often feels like something else. Something even more powerful. Something kingdoms have been lost for. It feels like…

2. Falling in Love: The Ultimate Drug Trip
Remember that I am discussing compatibility here. I am trying to show the way through the things that are mistaken for compatibility, in order to figure out what it really is.

Falling in love is so powerful, that when you fall for some-one, really fall, you don't even care if they love you back—you persist in your madness anyway. You actually feel that they *should* love you back, because you can't believe that what you are feeling could be wrong. If they stubbornly refuse to love you, you go and stand like John Cusack in the rain and hold up a boom box and play some romantic anthem like "Your Eyes" real loud outside their window, so that they will realize how sad, how *tragic* this miscarriage of justice is. (At least, you do this if you are a guy. If you are a woman you hole up with a cat and a pal like Joan Cusack and talk.)

Why is it a tragedy when "in love" isn't returned? Because lust is only about me, but "in love" is about the universe, it's about god. When you're in love, it feels as if you are tuned into the divine plan, the blueprint of eternity. Being in love equals believing that the two of you *were chosen* to mate, by the cos-mos, Destiny, a higher power. And what is mating about? It is about having babies, which is one of the toughest jobs in the world. That is why falling in love had to be made so fun. And that is why a man who falls in love may not be consciously thinking, "Babies: YES!" But when he looks in the eyes of his beloved, when she looks so right to him that is what his genes are thrilling to: *babies*.

What is he *consciously* thinking about? Well, he is probably thinking, "Oh, god she is beautiful. If only I can be worthy of her. She is too good for me, but I can't help trying. I'll never get her. She'll break my heart. But I have to try. I will try any-thing, I will make myself better, I will be whatever she wants me to be—just let me have her..." Or something like that. The fact is, a man is never so in love as when he feels undeserv-ing, when he is awestruck by the woman he has found. Even when she smiles upon him and holds his hand, he can hardly believe his good luck.

And you, when you are in love with a man, are you not thinking, "I have found the one, the chosen one, the one for me?"

That's the problem with falling in love. It seems to carry some seal of approval from the universe, that this person is perfect for you, that you and he are right in every way for each other.

Being in love carries with it *the illusion of compatibility*. That makes it very hard to ask, "In what ways are we actually compatible?" It makes the whole question seem irrelevant and ridiculous. Why worry about compatibility when love is all you need?

Unfortunately, Cupid is a drug dealer.

But unfortunately, Cupid is a drug dealer. Cupid alters our brain chemistry. He makes us swim in pheromones. Having clouded our minds, he heads us down the path to a broken heart. Or even if we take a kinder view, and say that falling in love is nature's best, sincerest try at finding soulmates and hooking them together, we have to admit: Too often, nature gets it wrong. We fall in love with the wrong people. (Or we fall in lust and think we are in love.) But even when we fall in vain, the intensity of the feeling reminds us of how badly we want the real thing, a real mate-for-life.

And when two people who really are right for each other find each other and get involved, nature will not fail to give them this feeling. Find the right person and love will find you. Find someone who is compatible with you. Fall in love with him. Then you will be in love forever.

Am I saying that *any* guy you are compatible with is someone you could fall for? If sexual chemistry is defined as part of compatibility, yes, I am.

Continuing my list of things often mistaken for compatibility, we come to:

3. Relationship Wishes: Delusions for Two

Many women define the man they are looking for in terms of his wanting the same things in a relationship that she does. This seems innocent enough but in fact is a snare and a delusion.

Phoebe is a hilarious woman in her thirties who says she has been unattached for a long time. On further questioning it emerges that she has had a series of unsatisfactory skirmishes with men that burned bright at the start and then fizzled like cheap fireworks.

I asked her what her philosophy is. What does she look for? She said she wants a guy who, when he's in a relationship, is bonded yet independent. Who is honest and isn't a game player. And who loves to laugh with his partner, not just with the boys.

And she finds men who "agree" with all these points. And they get together and it's great for a while, then it falls apart.

What is Phoebe getting wrong?

Well, the short answer is this: *Phoebe has defined Mr. Right in terms that almost every man would subscribe to.* So every attractive man she meets passes her test easily. Her criteria don't eliminate anyone.

Consider, if you were a guy chatting with an interesting woman, wouldn't you agree that the cool thing is to be bonded with your lover yet independent? Would any man admit to being a clingy wuss? Wouldn't you say you were honest? Does anyone on this planet claim to be dishonest? If you were a guy, would you say, "Oh, too bad, I'm a game player, I guess you wouldn't like me"? Would you say, "Gee, I don't like to share laughs with my girlfriend, it's too weird"? I don't think so.

And in fact, most men when giving these answers, would be telling the truth. Most men *think* they are honest, and funny, and not a game player, and capable of closeness-yet-independence.

So these are useless criteria.

They are expressions of a conventional formula. They don't separate anyone from anyone.

They are generic. They are clichés. Any halfwit with a pulse knows enough to agree with them.

But let's dig a little deeper. There is something else wrong with these criteria.

They focus on what type of *relationship* Phoebe seeks, not what type of man. Think about it. Everybody who is mature enough to interest us wants more or less the same kind of relationship. Everybody wants a partnership that is loving, sensual, touchy-feely but not too touchy-feely, full of good communication, sexy, fun, unpredictable, romantic, humorous, attached yet free, verbal yet quiet, loyal, trusting, faithful, and on and on.

But two people could both want all of this and yet have nothing in common.

Words like "honest, romantic, loyal, and trusting" characterize the relationship, not the individual.

To find Mr. Right, you have to get down to what makes him *different* from other people, the features that make him fit with one woman and not another. And the same goes for you.

We all want honesty. We all want warmth and closeness. We all want kisses that last forever.

We all want to be in love.

And we can get those things. *But first we have to find someone who has something in common with us, besides the mere desire for a nice relationship.*

In the next chapters we will find out what that means. Before we do that...

A NOTE ON TRUST

Trust is a beautiful thing when it exists between two people. It implies that they'll be loyal, they won't lie, they won't betray the other. For lovers it implies that they won't cheat.

The trouble with trust is that if you go looking for it—if you announce that trust or honesty is what you are seeking —that in no way guarantees that you will find it. In fact it probably hurts your odds. Let's see why.

Men are divided into those who try not to be dishonest (most of us), and those who *like* being dishonest. The latter group are the manipulators, the schemers, the guys who enjoy knowing something that their lover doesn't know, hoarding a secret that they realize would hurt their lover if she knew it. Sexually, they tend to be restless, hungry, always wanting the one they haven't had, and always losing interest once they've had her.

The problem is, if you carry a sign saying you are looking for honesty, are tired of game players, and are seeking a man you can trust—if you do this, you become liar-bait.

A dishonest man looks at you and says, "She is easy to fool; I know that, because she's been fooled before. Otherwise she wouldn't be so obsessed with honesty. She is needy; she so wants to be rescued from insecurity. She is gullible. All I have to do is snow her with a lot of 'honest' talk and she is mine."

The more you cross-examine such a man, the more you waste your energy; he knows what you want to hear, and he makes his living lying.

An honest man may not fare so well under your questioning. An honest man will admit that he lies sometimes; he may even admit that he cheated a time or two. If you take such a fanatical, absolutist position that you rule out any man who admits a few sins, you will be left only with the dishonest men. For they alone claim to have a perfect track record.

And that's not all. Let's take a look at a few hard truths about trust:

If you were a guy, would you say, "Oh, too bad, I'm a game player, I guess you wouldn't like me"?

Everyone lies. You know it and I know it. Learning to lie is part of becoming an adult. We try to honor what my old grandma told me: "If you can't say something nice, don't say anything at all." But that isn't good enough, because most of the time we have to say something! If we are asked a question and the true answer would hurt the other person's feelings, we make up a harmless lie. Especially if the defect is something that can't be easily changed. Children blurt out the truth and hurt others' feelings; adults guard each other from the truth. I won't bore you with examples; you can supply your own.

If you try to police your lover's thoughts or actions, you only drive them away. People are more likely to be happy in a couple when they feel free. If you constantly worry your man with your own fears that he will find a replacement for you, it becomes a self-fulfilling prophecy. If you are always watching him for telltale signs that he may find any other woman attractive; if you check his pockets and his phone bill and his e-mail; if you reveal your belief that he will stray unless your noble efforts prevent him—you are on the road to ruin. Because ultimately you are showing your own insecurity, your lack of self-esteem.

If on the other hand you radiate self-confidence; if he feels that you aren't worried about being replaced because you know darn well that you are irreplaceable, then he will come home relieved to have you.

Even honest lovers often cheat on their way to a new relationship. It's awful to say, but when you feel the first faint stirrings of love for a new person, you don't race off to your spouse and blurt out, "Guess what, I didn't mean to but I think I may have met someone who I am going to fall in love with and eventually leave you for."

Mary was a paediatric nurse, in a fairly miserable marriage with three kids. She and her husband both tried hard, but they just didn't enjoy each other anymore. Mary didn't usually go out much, she was too busy. But one day a couple of her co-workers dragged her to a local bar after work. There she struck up a conversation with Trevor, an IT guy who was there with some of his co-workers. Mary and Trevor hit it off on an emotional level: They found that they could really talk to each other, and they had similar feelings about their marriages. Mary went again with her friends; again she and Trevor ended up talking. They started looking forward to these late-afternoon meetings. They started to feel a little romantic.

Did Mary run to her husband and tell him there might be an interesting development? Of course not.

Did Mary lie about the visits to the bar? No.

Did she tell the *whole* truth? No. Why would she, when she didn't even know what this new thing was?

Did Mary and Trevor fall in love? Yes. Did they sneak off and have sex one afternoon? Yes. For both of them it was the first good sex they'd had in years.

Did Mary eventually come clean and tell her husband the truth? Yes. And they tried counselling, but to no avail. And she and Trevor both got divorces, and it was nasty and sad and difficult. And now they are together, married, and doing pretty well.

Mary and Trevor are among the honest ones. They didn't go looking to be unfaithful. They were both resigned to marriages from which the joy had been drained. But they encountered each other, by accident, and they couldn't turn away from the chance for love. They aren't dishonest people, and they hated having a dark secret. So as soon as they felt sure, they told the truth.

While we're on the subject, we should ask: Were Mary and Trevor honest before they met? The simple answer is no. Their marriages were lies.

Now I am obviously not recommending that you get involved with a married man. There are enough good unattached men out there that you never need to do that.

I was just making a point about trust.

If you search for absolute and perfect honesty, you will likely end up with a liar. *Honest men will admit their own imperfections.* Get to know a man, and see how he deals with life, and with you, and soon enough you will either feel comfortable with him or you won't.

COMPATIBILITY 201

Friendship with a Twist

$\mathcal{A}$ thought to ponder:

The couples who are happiest in this world are basically best friends who have the hots for each other.

If you think about the best friends you've had in your life —including your girlfriends—it may provide a guide to what makes friendship click for you. I think you'll find that you had a whole a lot of common ground in some crucial areas, and maybe you contrasted with each other in some others. The man you choose should rank right up there among the best friends you'll ever have.

A good general question is, would I want this person as a friend if we didn't have a sexual thing going?

Couples are also partners, running a very challenging enterprise called a family (with or without children). The best partnerships are yin-yang: People complement each other, they provide strengths where the other needs them. One may be better at organizing time, the other at handling money. One may be gregarious and fearless with people, the other may be better friends with blank sheets of paper that need to be filled with eloquent words. It's nice if you aren't always competing: Robin Williams was better off not marrying a comedian.

Another thought to ponder:

In the end all couples find themselves across a table from each other—whether it's in the kitchen at home or in a plaza in Italy. Pity those who have nothing to say.

One of the things that almost all great friendships have is good talk. Good friends love to converse. They don't get tired of talking, because they find each other's thoughts interesting. They bring different insights to the table, but they also are able to reach a consensus about important matters, so they don't end up always frustrated by disagreement.

They like to process experience together. They like to explore new territory, mental and physical.

When they travel, they enjoy it. Take a road trip with someone and you will quickly learn how well you really get along.

The old adage says, *Vive la difference.* You aren't looking for an opposite-sex clone of yourself (if such a thing could even exist). A clone would be predictable and irritating: The whole point of a relationship is to transcend oneself. Contrasts make the friendship exciting and challenging; they create a gap that keeps you respecting your friend's otherness.

But there are areas where a big gap can be very dangerous, where it is safer to be similar. Examples would be your fundamental values: politics, religion, morals. A lot of couples' misery can be easily explained by their reckless disregard of such differences.

Then there are areas where it isn't important that you be similar to each other, but it is important that you *fit together* well. For instance, body-type preferences. If you want tall and thin and he wants wide and curvy, that'll work out fine if you each fill the other's bill, but it certainly won't mean you are similar to each other. Sexually, many people hanker after someone who is an opposite body type. For starters, sperm-bearing humans mostly want egg-bearing humans (and it's mutual).

In the next few chapters I focus especially on areas that tend to be neglected or misunderstood. Along the way I also pay attention to these questions:

- Which things can you tell immediately about someone?
- Which things can you take his word for?
- Which things require that you get to know him and test them out by seeing how you two actually get along?

Sometimes I will go beyond compatibility. When you are trying to decide whether a man is mate material, some of the questions you will ask yourself are not about whether he is uniquely right for you. They're about whether he is right for anybody. Is he up to scratch in ways that any sane woman would want?

Would I want this person as a friend if we didn't have a sexual thing going?

It's an issue not of compatibility but of adequacy. But the issue is important and I include it in these compatibility chapters. It's an important part of vetting a man! In many cases what's happened is, you already met the guy, you like him, you're attracted to him, and now you're trying to detect whether he's the real thing. Is he a winner or a loser, has he got the goods in life? I cover several areas where this kind of question arises.

And now it's time for the grand tour of compatibility, and the first stop is the always-riveting topic of Personality.

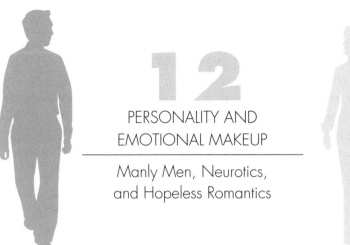

12

PERSONALITY AND EMOTIONAL MAKEUP

Manly Men, Neurotics, and Hopeless Romantics

*P*ersonality can be a silly term, evoking that perkiness which is so prized in Miss America contestants. Or it can have a sinister corporate ring to it, as in "personality tests" that corporations use to determine whom they shall employ and how they shall use those people. The notorious Myers-Briggs test is based on a breakdown of human beings into sixteen types that derives originally from the woolly speculations of Carl Jung. In recent years personality tests have been used by dating sites to predict which of us are good matches for each other. I have a lot to say about these tests in my discussion of eHarmony.com and other matchmaking sites in Part Three of this book.

As I've said before, I believe that the best way for you to "test" how your personality meshes with someone else's is for you to make your own observations when you two are interacting. Compatibility lives in the details and texture of your real time with another person. The trick, when you're getting to know someone, is to recognize clues when they appear—and that's why I am identifying them in these chapters. My goal is to provide a kind of anatomy of compatibility, so that when revealing moments happen, your antennae will be primed to detect them.

In this chapter I discuss four highly entertaining aspects of personality that are worth your attention: gender-rigidity; insecurities, neuroses, and complaints; attitude towards talking and sharing; and being romantic.

GENDER-RIGIDITY

Maybe this should be under values or even politics, rather than personality or attitude, but the point is, there is an issue that will send up quiet but important signals during your months of getting to know a new man. It has to do *with how rigidly you each define masculinity and femininity*. The two of you need to be equally flexible (or rigid), or there will be trouble.

Some women expect a man to live up to a traditional stereotype of masculinity and vice versa. Others have a looser standard, and don't mind it if the genders trade a lot of roles. If you find that a man seems to regularly violate your own code of what manliness is, or if he hints that you offend his vision of what is feminine, you had better look for a different man, because in the long run, personal respect and sexual compatibility will be at risk.

Clare Kent and Her Boyfriends

Clare Kent was thirty-four when Lorne Lang struck up a conversation with her at the McMichael art gallery in Kleinburg, north of Toronto. Lorne liked the Group of Seven and Clare liked Tom Thomson's paintings, so they were off to a great start. What made her delicious to him was that she was very girly, with her pale summer dress, her slender body, and her blonde bangs. She even had a pleasing high voice.

As for Clare, she liked Lorne's dark eyes, his smile, and his almost military bearing; and she liked the fact that he cared about paintings. Although his pants and short-sleeved shirt had a J.C. Penney look that struck her as kind of uptight, his body looked lean and firm.

And he was aggressive.

So aggressive, in fact, that they ended up necking in front of an A.Y. Jackson canvas, and then they went to Lorne's place and made oily love on his couch.

On their next date an odd thing happened. Lorne insisted on holding the door open for her while she walked out of the house. The problem was, it was her house (a renovated red brick in the Islington area) and she needed to close the door and lock it, but he stood awkwardly in her way, as if doors were his exclusive bailiwick.

He drove them to an Italian restaurant and took twenty minutes to find street parking on Eglinton, even though a parking lot was beckoning. During this exercise Clare noticed a wheezing noise coming from the engine of Lorne's Camry, and told him he might be low on oil. He gave her an offended look and said, "I just had the oil changed." After he finally parked the car, Lorne raced around to open Clare's door before she could even get her seat belt unhooked. By the time they got to the restaurant Clare had had enough. She delivered a clean body check so that she could open the door for herself.

Things improved over dinner and wine and their natural sexual chemistry kicked in again. They held hands and stared into each other's eyes and agreed to go camping two weeks later—just a weekend jaunt to Algonquin Park, where they could admire some of the fall colours that the Group of Seven had captured so well.

It was on the camping trip that Clare's secret identity was revealed. Far from the mild-mannered, soft girl of Lorne's dreams, she was in fact... handy.

She was very handy.

They took her car, an old Honda, because it had a rack to haul her cedar-strip canoe, and because Lorne's Camry was in the shop with a burnt-out engine. At a rest stop on the 400 the car wouldn't start, and Lorne stared helplessly in the sun until Clare pulled a metal pole out of the trunk and told him to turn the ignition key. She jammed the pole into the alternator and the car started. "It does that sometimes," she said.

As the weekend progressed, Lorne watched Handy Woman do everything better than he could. She drove like a NASCAR ace; she told excellent dirty jokes; she was very good in the woods. She could pitch a tent in ten minutes and scale a fish in five. She was afraid of snakes, but this didn't help because Lorne was too.

To Clare's puzzlement, Lorne became more and more withdrawn. He seemed hurt like a little boy. He gave up on paddling in the stern and said, "Why don't you do it" in a bitter voice. He didn't like his fish dinner.

Nothing happened in the sleeping bag that night. Clare tried to encourage him but he was as limp as he was silent.

After the long drive home, they never saw each other again.

But that was okay because Clare met a new beau, Lonnie Lane, a cardiac nurse who was no good at anything except cooking and cardiac nursing. But unlike the unfortunate Lorne,

Lonnie delighted in Clare's every ability, liking to sit back and admire her exploits, singing her praises and not hesitating to pitch in where he could. She couldn't hold a candle to him in the kitchen, but she took care of everything else. And oh, their meals were five-star celebrations. Lonnie was good at one other thing: He was very resourceful in bed, and there they both gave no quarter and asked none.

Was Lonnie more masculine than Lorne? No. In fact, word on the street has it that these two men were equally masculine. But not equally secure. Lonnie was easygoing about his masculinity, and equally easygoing about women's gender-identity. Lorne was uptight and rigid about what a man should be and what a woman should be. Lorne needed to be with a woman as rigid as he was, though one wonders who would fix the car.

It's good to find someone who shares your style of neurosis. The root problem with Lorne is that he doesn't live up to his own image of what a man should be. Lorne isn't good with cars, canoes, or snakes. Lorne has a problem even before he gets with a woman—he is inadequate in his own eyes. But a woman's presence ups the ante for him—she could mean exposure, or even humiliation, if she outdoes him in any area that he deems to be properly male. That is why Lorne tries to adhere to a rigid code of masculine manners, and that is why he wants a woman to be rigidly confined to a feminine persona.

So when you find yourself thinking, "Boy, he sure is masculine," make sure you aren't confusing rigidity with masculinity. A man who makes a big deal out of how masculine he is, and who seems to want to enforce a strict code of how "gentlemen" and "ladies" behave, may be masking insecurity.

INSECURITIES, NEUROSES, AND COMPLAINTS

Gender identity was just one example. In any aspect of human character, rigidity is a sign of insecurity.

But it doesn't necessarily follow the other way around: Insecurity doesn't have to lead to rigidity. It depends on how a person deals with their insecurity. The equation goes something like this:

Insecurity + dishonesty = rigidity

Lorne's deepest problem is lack of honesty. That which he hides from himself, he has to forbid others to see. Someone who is honest about his problem—who can laugh about it and admit that he is insecure—is less likely to inflict it on someone else by being rigid, judgmental, or intolerant.

And that raises an interesting question. If you are a somewhat neurotic person, is it better for you to be with someone who is also that way? I'm not talking about serious mental illness here: I will leave that to the experts. I'm talking about everyday quirks and problems that many viable people have. And my opinion is that it's often good to find someone who shares your general level of neurosis, if not your particular foibles. Or, maybe I should say, someone who shares your style of neurosis. Being neurotic myself, I'm suspicious of those who claim not to be neurotic at all. It's just that different people have different . coping strategies, and some of them clash pretty badly within the walls of a relationship.

Worriers and Warriors

Take anxiety. Some people have more than a fair share of it. Faced with everyday challenges, they worry a lot about what may go wrong; they go through a rollercoaster of emotions on the way to coping with a tough situation. In the end they may cope very well, and in fact their worrying may enable them to avoid pitfalls that might ambush a more secure person.

It isn't helpful for a true worrier to be with a warrior, a person who dismisses all worries as silly, and who soldiers through all adversity, refusing to admit any qualms. True worriers need to vent anxieties, and have them listened to with respect: That is how they process oncoming events and cope with them. Some reassurance can be a good thing, but having your feelings scoffed at, dismissed, or downright denied is not.

So it's probably best when two people are at roughly the same level of mental health, so that they can understand what the other person is going through, and can empathize and comfort in a way that isn't condescending. If I'm all tied up in knots about a job interview I have to go through tomorrow, it's wonderful if my lover looks at me and nods, "Oh god, I know exactly how you feel. I was terrified when I had to interview for the web designer position... I know I'm good, and yet I feel like a fraud."

Venting annoyance or outrage is one of life's genuine pleasures. The first thing that professional counsellors are taught is the value of acknowledging. When you spill your fears to your partner, the most helpful thing he can do is, *not try to help*. Instead, it would be nice if he would listen attentively and let you know that the way you feel makes sense to him, that it rings true. Most people can sort out their *own* fears and worries if they are given a legitimate chance to voice their concerns.

So whether you are a star worrier or not, pay attention to what happens on occasions when you are discouraged or anxious and you try to talk to your new guy about it. If the conversation flows freely, and you are not hampered from expressing what you are feeling and thinking, that is good. But if you feel censored, and you end up frustrated instead of feeling better, that is a good clue that this guy is not a match for you.

Complainers v. Positive Thinkers:
To Vent is Human

As we've seen, not all negativity is neurotic. In fact a lot of it is darn healthy. Here's another example.

Ann would get home from a day working as Charlotte's helper. She would often be tired and down, with good reason. Charlotte was a crusty gal who had given Ann work as a house painter. Ann needed the work badly, but she really didn't need to be working with someone like Charlotte: a rage-filled woman who got so wrapped up in her frustration with every stiff roller and every spackle crack, that she couldn't provide a sane space in which her helper could actually help. Ann was forever getting spattered by Charlotte's war with Charlotte. On top of that, when Ann had a nice pleasant job to do, like painting a new bathroom cabinet, Charlotte would somehow find time to oversee it, which usually meant trying to take over. Some days went okay when the two women worked mostly in separate rooms, but many days didn't.

So Ann would get home, and if it had been a bad day, she naturally needed to vent her frustrations. Unfortunately the person Ann needed to vent to was Colin, whom she'd met six months earlier and had just started living with.

Colin, who had had a somewhat pampered journey, had a philosophy about life, that you must always be positive. It's all good. Dwelling on unpleasant facts will only lead to pain. Complaining or expressing anger is a stain on an always-sunny day and it must be wiped clean.

So Colin would contradict every point Ann made, with pseudo-kindness.

Ann would say, "Charlotte outdid herself today. She actually tried to tell me how to unscrew a knob on a cabinet."

Colin would reply, "Well, maybe she really cares about how that is done."

So it would go. Ann, who was actually a hilarious raconteur especially when irritated, never got to raconte. She never got to vent. She would eventually just stop trying, feeling even more bottled up than when she'd started.

And what was bottled up was the truth. Colin couldn't handle the truth.

Jealousy is about the rival, not about the loved one. We have a complete right to articulate things that are wrong and bad and unfair and annoying that we have encountered, had our noses rubbed in, or otherwise detected. Venting annoyance or outrage is one of life's genuine pleasures; sometimes the only relief against those things that suck is putting them into clear, eloquent words. And sometimes those words are the first step towards dealing with the problem.

So, if you know you are a venter, don't choose a partner who reacts to healthy venting by trying to squelch it. Choose one who gets it, who knows how to aid and abet you in skewering the awful stuff.

Inferiority is Not Nutritious

We were talking a moment ago about insecurities: How about feeling threatened by your partner's fabulousness? The human ego is a tricky thing. We can be inspired by those who excel at what we want to do; but a steady diet of inferiority is not conducive to growth. If there's an arena that you feel weak in (for example, you're not very good at public speaking, but you're trying hard to improve in that area), and if you're constantly with someone who easily does better than you, it could just paralyze you and hold you back.

Respect is good; feeling threatened by someone else's prowess is not so good. So watch out for this distinction when you are getting to know a man. Look for a *balance* of prowesses, that can sustain mutual respect over time. If one person consistently feels inferior or insecure, we don't have a match. If you are the one feeling inferior, don't be fooled by the argument that "I can't let his good qualities be a problem; I have no right to feel bad because he is so great."

Find someone you feel equal to.

Insecurity Masquerading as Possessiveness

Some men and women think it their job to police their partner's activities and limit their freedom to interact with other people, especially members of the opposite sex.

Now some jealousy is natural and even lovable, but when jealousy seeks to stop an innocent person from being themselves, it becomes a form of abuse.

It is especially insidious when the real problem lies with the jealous party.

I had an epiphany a long time ago, when I found the key to my own jealousy over a girl I was in love with. There was another guy in our circle whom I saw that she liked, and it was driving me crazy. Then one day when it was too late I realized that the whole reason for my jealousy had been that I was afraid (with good reason) that he was a more impressive person than I was. The insight I had was that *jealousy is about the rival, not about the loved one. It's about feeling threatened by the rival*. I was lacking in self-confidence, had a shaky opinion of myself, and that was the source of the problem. If I had believed that I was just as good as the other guy, my situation would have lost its sting. But I was threatened by him, and that was why her (platonic) interest in him was so painful to me.

By the time I saw the truth, I had lost her.

The only solution to such scenarios is for the jealous person to admit that it is his problem, not his partner's problem. And that is not easy to achieve, because it involves bitter self-knowledge.

So if a man seems to be starting a campaign of limiting your social contacts from what they would naturally be, look long and hard at the situation.

ATTITUDE TOWARDS TALKING AND SHARING

Donna and Brantley had a strange time together during their engagement. Donna liked to check in with Brantley about twenty times a day, just to say hey and find out what snack food he was munching. During these brief calls she would give him tantalizing previews of the ongoing saga called "How my day is unfolding."

They both worked but her job was easily interruptible. Brantley's wasn't. He liked to forget about personal stuff while he was doing his demanding job in law. And he liked to be away from Donna—really away from her—so he could miss her and work up a yen to see her again. Because they were frothy with amour and hardly knew each other and had gotten engaged on a crazy day when they happened to drive past a wedding party, he tried his best to accommodate her many phone calls, and her impulsive visits to his workplace.

And he almost made it. But at the end of the day, when they were together at a meal or in bed, Donna reached her favourite moment: the moment when she could finally tell him in rich, analytical detail the story of every single thing that had happened to her that day! Donna was actually a lively and colourful narrator, but after a few weeks of this, Brantley just had to give up. The engagement ended.

For the awful truth about Brantley was that he really didn't like to listen. He occasionally enjoyed talking and being listened to with appreciation, but the job of switching his ears to *on* and keeping them like that for minutes or even hours was just too tough. Especially when the topic was, "and then she said bla bla bla and I couldn't believe it and so I called Brenda and asked her what she thought and right then Lars walked into my office with lattes and so I'm having two conversations at once and...and...and..."

Mates tell stories to each other about what they've seen, heard, and experienced—about what happened to them today and what happened long ago. If you look at happy couples, you'll find that they both enjoy hearing the other one tell a story. They don't interrupt it or grow impatient with it. They let the other one tell it at a suitable level of detail because they enjoy it.

If you find your date's stories annoying, in any of various ways—not funny, boring, too long, too disjointed, too superficial, in bad taste, and many more!—that's a bad sign. Consider moving on.

BEING "ROMANTIC"

"I am a hopeless romantic," a woman says to a man.

"Really?" he replies, "So am I!"

This statement and fifty cents won't even get you a coffee these days. So don't trust it.

Men and women mean two different things by "romantic."

Men mean, "When I splurge on dinner I bring you roses too." Or, "On those rare occasions when I figure out that you are really mad at me, I know how to pile on the frills." Or, just to give some men their due, they mean, "When we are having a really special, sexy, second-honeymoon kind of an evening, and you are sporting great cleavage in a black nightgown, I will order up champagne and candlelight—or in other words, *I know how to pile it on.*"

Women mean, "When you are away from me, you think about me all the time, and you do thoughtful little things to let me know."

In other words, for men, romantic means, "How I act (rarely) when I am with you"; and for women, romantic means, "How you act when you are not with me." Let's face it, traditionally the mating female's greatest fear is that her male will stray. Especially after she has given him what he wanted (her body). When she has nothing further to offer but responsibilities and rug rats, he will wander to the next princess who seems to offer only sensual delights (no chores). So of course, what she appreciates most is a man who thinks of her, who misses her, who longs for her, *in her absence.*

A romantic man *calls.* After the first night that you sleep with him, he calls to tell you.... What? How great the sex was? No. He calls to tell you how much he values you. A good phrase might be, "I love you." Unfortunately, that is a little hard to say after the first sleepover, so what is a gallant swain to do? He sends you a card, or flowers, or a little gift (maybe something with a special meaning to the two of you). Because he is a big tuff man, he tells you in a symbol, 'cause his manly lips can't form the words yet. (Or ever.) Whenever you are apart, he thinks of you and he lets you know in these clever little ways. In other words, what makes him romantic is that he feels the same way you do, but being manly, he can't express it as easily, so he has to resort to symbolism. Being romantic is about *manliness trying to cope with its feminine side*.

Most men think they are romantic, because they don't know what it means.

So if a man tells you he is a hopeless romantic, don't say to yourself, "Oh! I am a hopeless Romantic too! That must mean we are compatible!" Instead, get to know him for a while. See what he actually does when you are apart.

We move now to a topic that is important and sadly neglected; the so-called experts are very shallow about it. I'm talking about sense of humour.

SENSE OF HUMOUR

The Fingerprint of the Soul

*P*lease believe me, humour is way more important than most people think it is.

But I am not saying, find a man who has a "good" sense of humour. I am not saying that.

What I *am* saying is, notice whether the things he laughs at bother you. And vice versa. And notice whether the things you think are funniest, make him laugh too...

Humour is the fingerprint of the human soul.

In its origins, humour is a tribal ritual. A shared catharsis about how screwed-up the world is, and the people in it. It is a group of people sharing the vision of their own failings, which are not quite terrible enough to threaten the group's survival. Humour demands your assent. You sit in a movie theatre and the person next to you finds something funny, and they look at you to get your agreement; they *need* you to go along. Because it's a form of bonding—a group sport. That is why sitcoms have a laugh track—to create the illusion that the rest of the tribe is already laughing, thus leaving the viewer no choice. Which is why some people cannot stand sitcoms.

And that is why there is nothing more alienating than being in a group that is gripped by hilarity, when you yourself don't find the thing funny. It means you are a pariah, you don't belong, you are alone. *Humour presupposes a world view.* If you don't agree with that world view, you are out.

At its best, humour is us laughing at us. It frees us from pride and vanity, it frees us from hypocrisy, humour lets us see the awful truth while bringing us the comfort of facing it together: Humour allows us to forgive ourselves for what we are. At its worst, humour is *us* laughing at *him or her*: one person being humiliated and isolated by the laughter of a group.

What is amazing is that such an animalistic braying can be triggered by the most subtle, refined twist of thought.

Humour is a very primitive physical response, undignified in its bodily explosion, an orgasm of insight that causes an ejaculation of noise accompanied by facial expressions and gestures that mimic ecstasy and pain. What is amazing is that such an animalistic braying can be triggered by the most subtle, refined twist of thought. Or by Three Stooges slapstick.

What a person laughs at can signal their uniqueness and originality. It can also be an index of their deepest values. It is a measure of their heart, their soul, and their mind. Traveller, ignore its signposts at your peril.

TWO NOT-SO-FUNNY STORIES

Sandra and Jim were married with kids. They put on a fine show of normality and wholesomeness; they were careful, conscientious parents. There was one fatal sign, however. If you spent any time with them you would notice it: Jim frequently tried to crack jokes that made Sandra cringe. She was embarrassed by his idea of humour. Like racial jokes: If an anecdote mentioned an East Indian, Jim was sure it was hilarious. Sandra didn't find this funny. After a decade together, Jim had learned to crack these jokes in a furtive way, almost guiltily, like a dog who knows he's doing something forbidden but just can't restrain himself. This only made things worse. It drew attention to his gaucheness. Sandra had to shake off these moments, try to pretend that they weren't happening. Later she would snap at him or say something to hurt him, because of the discomfort he had caused her.

What was going on here was a clash of world views, a clash of values. Important values: moral values. Jim had just enough class to not make *serious* comments against foreigners, but he could not keep the tip of that iceberg from showing in his humour. The fact was, he thought of foreigners as inferior and ridiculous *because they were "different."* He thought his corner of the world was the center of it all. He didn't hate foreigners, but he was a smug bigot nonetheless.

And this was only one example of how his humour rubbed Sandra the wrong way. His jokes, even when they were not bigoted, tended to be heavy-handed. He didn't know how to be subtle. He telegraphed his points—and they were already obvious to begin with. Sandra came from a family background where humour was more elegant, smarter. Jim's attempts at humour rubbed Sandra's nose in the fact that he was not as bright as she needed him to be.

Sexually, things had dried up between them years ago. And here is an interesting fact: If you had asked Sandra what had made her turn off from Jim sexually, her answer would have been, "He assumes that he's the center of it all. He doesn't pick up on the fine signals. He is too heavy-handed." Hmm... doesn't that sound a lot like a description of his sense of humour?

Sandra eventually split with Jim, and her years of barely suppressed anger were ended.

And their doom could be read all along, in the handwriting on the wall of Humour.

Consider Richard and Gail. Gail was a bit of a clown, known among her friends for her boundless, fearless sense of humour. She was always doing shtick, creating a lot of it herself—she was a keen observer of the human scene and a clever mimic. Her best friends would sometimes gather around her and just sit back, letting her riff, howling with delight. Richard, however, was a stiffer sort. In his own head, he had to forgive Gail for her shenanigans before he could let himself commit to her. He was a cautious, colder soul, very protective of his own dignity. Worst of all, he did not laugh at Gail's best stuff. *He didn't think she was funny.* (If he had, maybe she could have brought him out of his proud isolation.)

A few years later, Gail was not funny any more. Her friends still loved her, but they didn't see much of her, and they missed her old spirit.

When a man laughs unexpectedly, make sure you find out why.

For Gail had become an abused wife. Richard had turned out to be very protective, jealous, controlling. And very threatened by Gail. In order to counter this threat, he had to reduce her to less than she was, had to kill the playfulness in her. When she tried to be herself, he skilfully shared with her what was wrong with that self. So she learned. Learned too well.

But one day she ran into her old friend Jean, and they had a drink and Gail laughed about her marriage until she cried, and she remembered who she was. After that she fought back and she left Richard.

And now she makes her friends laugh, but the humour is even edgier and darker than before.

The general point here is this. When you are checking out a new guy, wondering if he may be Mr. Right, don't treat humour as a trivial diversion. Treat it as an important clue to compatibility. *Because humour is such an instinctive thing, it is hard to fake.* People calculate a lot of their moves, but humour tends to be less planned. So it is more revealing.

When a man laughs unexpectedly, make sure you find out why. It may be bad news, or it may be wonderful news. Sometimes it will trigger a surprising revelation, open a window on his soul.

A phony laugh is one of the best clues there is that the laugher is a phony person.

Jokes are not always the best tool for getting to know an individual.

A man who inhibits your sense of humour may not be the man for you. When you try to communicate a point that to you is hilarious, and you feel him draw back or he just doesn't get it—that is a sign that all is not well. *Even worse*, if you begin to edit your own material, altering your personality to suit him, beware.

Can he laugh at himself? If he does something dumb and you satirize it perfectly, does he dissolve into life-threatening laughter and beg for mercy? If so, score one for the two of you. If his pride won't let you mock his weak points, look out. A man who needs to sustain a too-perfect image of himself, will need you to help him sustain it. And that will mean that you'll have to lie, you'll be increasingly trapped in a pretend world, and you'll become afraid of the truth, like he is. *Never forget that laughter is your right.* No one can tell you what is or isn't funny—your deepest identity depends on it.

Humour is also a very important survival mechanism, and it can get couples through some rough times. It can allow them to shake off all the serious and heavy issues that make modern life so stressful. You've got to share each other's struggles and dreams, but it's even better if, in the middle of sweating blood over some precious goal, you can look at each other and start laughing.

Taste in humour matters. If he likes sitcoms and you don't; if your favourite comedy of all time left him cold; if your best witticisms seem to fly right past him—these are warning signs, red flags that indicate differences in values, intelligence, and perception.

JOKES

Sense of humour is often confused with a love of jokes. The two are related, but they aren't the same. Jokes are weird. Some people relish jokes and some don't. Some people collect them, remember them, and repeat them. Others, if asked, would not be able to remember a single joke. Jokes are canned humour. In the hands of a master, they are an art form. In other hands they can be an extreme nuisance. There is nothing quite as squirm-inducing as hearing someone launch into what you know is going to be a long-winded joke, when you aren't in the mood, or know they don't make you laugh. You become a trapped audience, all other conversation has to cease, and you feel manipulated and put-upon because not only do you have to suffer through the whole story, but also you are expected to laugh at the end.

Jokes are, by their very nature, impersonal. They are like a form of currency, passed on from person to person, waves that move through our culture. They essentially belong to no one, and to everyone. For that reason they are not always the best tool for getting to know an *individual*. You can sit with a man all evening and be entertained by his endless supply of jokes— and you may have learned nothing about him! Men who have the nervous habit of telling a million jokes are often trying to hide. Trying to use public coinage because they are afraid of how little they have to offer of a private, personal nature. In particular, they may fear that they have no sense of humour.

That is why many people prefer spontaneous humour: one-liners, witticisms, zingers. Or you may find that someone is funniest when he isn't even trying to be funny, but is just being bluntly honest. The relief of hearing the truth (usually about some awful thing we all share) makes you howl with laughter.

"I love to laugh," a man may say in describing himself to a possible mate. "Therefore, I'm looking for someone who loves to laugh."

To which a woman may answer, "At what? Do you think *everything* is funny?"

SEXUAL COMPATIBILITY

The Six Factors that Determine
a Couple's Chances

Some people are good in bed, some aren't. If you are good in bed, find someone else who is. If you aren't, pray.

Not so much. Like most aspects of human life, sex is relative. A man who does you no good in bed may be just what someone else ordered. And vice versa. Nevertheless, if a man seems to you to be a bad lover, then for you he is.

It's all about how two people click.

Let's assume that you click as people: that you have the potential to be really good friends. Then six factors will determine your fate as lovers.

THE SIX FACTORS IN SEXUAL COMPATIBILITY

1. Attraction
Before you ever touch someone's hand, even before you meet in person, attraction can make itself felt. Look through a hundred photos on a dating site and you'll find that a few of them catch you and hold you, make you want to see more. Talk to

a man on the phone and find out what his voice does to you. Be with a man in person, and if you enjoy looking at him, hearing his voice, if you like his scent—and if these things are mutual—you're off to the races.

If the other sexual factors also turn out right, these early sources of attraction will keep on giving you enjoyment indefinitely. When just watching your partner move around a room gives you pleasure, you have a lot of pleasure in store.

2. Interaction: kissing, cuddling, stroking, touching, feeling, tasting, and smelling.

Sometimes two people find each other devastatingly attractive, and then they kiss and it fizzles. How can this be?

The Two Types of Good Kisser

Well, you won't read this in Dr. Phil's dating book, but there are two types of good kisser in the world. (There are also twenty-seven types of bad kisser, which we won't discuss.)

We've been told that men are from Mars and women from Venus. Well, that turns out to be not quite right. Thanks to groundbreaking research in several fields for which I will take credit, it is now clear that, at least as regards Kissing Men and Kissing Women, there are two other orbiting bodies in play. And every man and woman comes from one or the other.

The first type of good kisser is from the planet Neptune. Neptune was of course the god of the sea, and a Neptune kisser will take you to the depths, very quickly. The other type of good kisser hails from Ariel, which happens to be the twelfth satellite of the planet Uranus. Ariel was an airy spirit in Shakespeare's *The Tempest*, and if you like to float above things before you touch down, you may well be an Ariel kisser. Both types are valid, or I wouldn't have called them *good* kissers, and both have a right to exist according to psychologists and astronomers. But if you are one type, be very wary of teaming up with the other. If you have ever felt baffled by what some men are doing when they kiss you, read on.

What are these types?

Well, a Neptune kisser is *mouth and tongue* oriented right from the start, and is engaged in a cagey exploration that is soft, wet, tongue-y, and teasing. The hidden message in a good Neptune kiss—and they are all good, we said that—is, "I am already exploring the depths of your body and mind, already engaged in the dive of sex with you, and sending you waterproof photos of the delights and challenges that lie in store for you if we take this all the way down." Neptune kisses are thought by some experts to be properly subsumed under what is called "scuba sexuality"; whereas Ariel kissers are thought of more as snorkelers on the surface of ecstasy. But let it be said right now in defence of snorkellers that they can and do go deep when they want to, without the aid of special equipment.

You won't read this in Dr. Phil's dating book, but there are two types of good kisser in the world.

Now for the Ariel kisser. An Ariel kisser is *lip* oriented at the start—that's *open* lip, by the way, no tight-mouthed puritans in this club—and wants a nice fit, with pressure that starts off gentle but as it gets more passionate, answers firmness with firmness, and doesn't get tongue-y or wet right away because that would distract from the thrilling sensation of lip cells in contact. Moist yes, wet no. Only in the throes of passion does the Ariel snorkeller really move on to tongue, and even then it is not with the same dedication as the Neptune diver. The hidden message in a good Ariel kiss is, "You're beautiful, I'm falling in love with you." If it evolves into something more like a Neptune kiss, its message becomes more redolent of seaweed and pearls. (The fact that the one style can seamlessly flow into the other is very inconvenient for theorists, so we put it in parentheses.)

We've been told that men are from Mars and women from Venus. Well, that turns out to be not quite right.

When people of the two types try to kiss, they frustrate each other. To begin with, they may not even be able to get their heads tilted right. Ariel will want the heads to be forming the classic X like in the movies—at right angles to each other—so that the lips can meet without noses in the way. Neptune doesn't care as much about this, because he is not into geometry. Ariel, if she can achieve a nice meeting of the lips, will then press more firmly, only to find that Neptune gives way, beginning his classic tease. Meanwhile Neptune will be wondering why his tongue is being ignored... and so it goes.

People of both types will claim with total authority that so-and-so is a great kisser, and so-and-so isn't—but their choices will exactly conflict.

I won't talk about bad kissers: For example, the type described by a girl I knew in high school. After a date with a new guy, she said that his good night kiss consisted of completely engulfing her mouth in his, in a sort of death trap... but he was a good dancer.

We're talking about sexual interaction as part of compatibility. Sexual interaction ranges from kissing to everything two people do to each other; but we're not talking yet about *which things* they choose to do—we're talking about whether you like *the way the other person does things*. It's about style. Do you like the way he touches you? Is it annoyingly tentative, or too hard? Or is it just right? Is it arousing and sensual, does it make you feel beautiful? Does he react when you touch him?

There is the olfactory essence of someone. When you sink your nose into the place where his neck meets his shoulder, do you like the smell of his molecules?

And there is rhythm. When two people do almost anything sexually, even when one is giving and the other is receiving, either the rhythm will come together so the two people can sync up with each other and build to a crescendo, or it will keep getting lost and they will fall out of the moment. Finding that someone shares your sense of rhythm is like winning the lottery.

When you sink your nose into the place where his neck meets his shoulder, do you like the smell of his molecules?

Finally, there is technique. In our prowess-driven culture, sex is sometimes treated as if it all comes down to technique. But technique really has little to do with compatibility, for one simple reason. Technique can be taught. If you like the look, feel, and smell of someone, his kiss and his touch, it is very possible that he can learn to please you in many ways that he doesn't yet know. And vice versa: You can learn the special things that drive him mad. How? Well, by experimenting and by communicating.

But if you are not compatible in the areas that can't be taught, technique is unlikely to bail you out.

3. Coachability, Generosity, Desire to Please

Many women and men know what they want, what unique

moves can be counted on to please them sexually. But this won't do them any good if their partner doesn't want to hear about it.

You could have all the other factors going with a man, but if you don't have ability and willingness to learn, you've got a problem. If he thinks he already knows everything, and he won't let you teach him what you like; if he feels demeaned by any coaching you offer, as if it insults him as a lover...

Trouble.

Probably one of the most attractive features another person can have is desire to please, accompanied by desire to learn *what* pleases. It may seem like a submissive thing, but it isn't necessarily. A partner who learns how to arouse and satisfy you, and then generously offers you those things when the time is ripe, can also learn to enjoy the power that gives them.

4. Agenda

Where do you each want sex to go, what activities do you want it to include?

Sex can be thought of in various ways, for example:

- A sensual picnic on the landscape of each other's bodies;
- A siege of a provocative fortress with a turgid battering ram;
- A performance at the Theatre of Power and Pain;
- A Valentine that leads to orgasm;
- A chance to scratch an itch.

Maybe it's all these things and more, for a couple who are versatile and flexible enough. Or maybe it's just some of them: If so, he and she had better agree on which ones. If you can't really get off unless your partner talks dirty to you, you're not going to be happy with a man who hates to get verbal while getting it on. The only way to find out is to talk about it or try it: Just because you like someone a lot in non-sexual ways doesn't mean that you want to go to the same places in bed.

People have fantasies, and sometimes they want to talk about them, and sometimes they want to really live them out. A lot of people never get that chance, because they are afraid to reveal their secret dreams, or because they sense that their partner doesn't want them to. Some fantasies turn out to be best left as fantasies: When you try to do them they dissolve into humour or bad theatre. And some fantasies come to life, because both people "get" them, and they take on enormous power, to where they can give deep pleasure and expose sensitive layers of the psyche. It's wise to explore these things if you're getting serious about someone. Find out what riches may be waiting in the shadows, and find out if any deal-breakers are lurking there too.

Maybe your kink is already highly developed. If so you have probably already learned how to locate partners who can supply the other half of what you're into. Even among the incorrigibly kinky, there may be two camps: Those who are into "the life" and have found a home in an established subculture with all of its accepted costumes and rituals; and those who want to invent their own original journey, tailored to their own unique psyches, and who reject anything conventional or conformist.

Look into your soul, see which one you are and want.

5. Duration and Stamina (And Foreplay, Intercourse, and Orgasm)

How much total time do you typically like to devote to a sexual encounter? How long should foreplay last? How long intercourse? Men and women can be wired a little differently in these regards: Have you and your partner found common ground?

Speaking of orgasm, which we should, there are women who want to climax from intercourse, and who require it to last a long time in order to reach that point. Are you one of them, and does your prospective partner fill the bill?

Or, would you say that as long as intercourse is artful and intense, it needn't be of Olympic duration? Could that be partly because you want lots of orgasms but intercourse *isn't* how you get there? *Other* activities are the way, and they aren't exactly "foreplay," because that word implies intercourse is the end goal. But it isn't, always. And maybe the whole notion of stamina needs another look...

Marvin v. Fred: Cynthia Gets Down with Stamina

Cynthia melted the first time Marvin held her in his arms. He'd come over to her table at the Blues Bar as "Stormy Monday" was starting, and asked her to dance. He was tall, rugged, assured. She didn't like dancing to fast stuff but this song was slow and she said yes. As they danced, they hit it off when they were talking, and they bonded even more deeply when they weren't. They ended up dancing all night, even to the up-tempo numbers.

They dated for a while and then they went to bed. Marvin did not disappoint. He was a skilled lover and he could go on forever. As far as intercourse was concerned, this guy was Stamina Stud. Cynthia was impressed; Cynthia had to admire his performance. But admiration can only take you so far. It left one small problem: She didn't get to come. She didn't think this was necessarily Marvin's fault. It's me, she told herself. I need to get there a different way.

And he did try. He did bring other methods (manual and oral) to bear, and she would get started on the way to her pinnacle, but then he would stop, after only ten minutes. She even tried to coach him. But it seemed the challenge was too great. Marvin just couldn't last. This kind of stamina he didn't have.

She thought, Some men will do what pleases them for as long as I want; other men will do what pleases me for as long as it takes.

Then Cynthia met Fred in a laundromat. Fred was rumpled, buggy-eyed, and very funny in a self-deprecating way. They had a coffee. She liked him and he was totally unthreatening, so impulsively she went to his one-room apartment and they listened to Coldplay and lounged on his bed.

After a while they were cuddling, and then he started to touch her and she felt an electric charge move up her spine and she drew a sharp breath and just surrendered.

Fred didn't need any coaching. He was very creative and dedicated in this area. She didn't feel like he was showing off his skill, it was more like this was his way of loving her body. Before she was really expecting it she started to hit ledges of intensity that made her feel like the mountaintop was within reach. Then he would tease her, make her ache for the next step, then give it to her. At the twenty-minute mark she began to climax and it rolled on in waves for a goodly time.

And Cynthia thought, "That's interesting. *Some men will do what pleases them for as long as I want; other men will do what pleases me for as long as it takes.* Okay, maybe there are different types of stamina." She didn't end up having a serious relationship with Fred; they were sporadic friends for a while. But she did add four things to her list of important sexual virtues: patience, dedication, generosity, and inventiveness.

6. Frequency: A scientific-sounding word hiding a Pandora's Box of fascinating issues.

Nature seems to have stacked the deck so that men and women will have trouble agreeing on how often they should have sex. Men, we are told, reach their sexual peak at age eighteen. Women reach theirs at age forty. (Some experts disagree, but Pandora isn't one of them.)

That means men are going to want sex more often than women, until some crossover age is reached, and after that women will want it more. A sorry plight for the already "threatened" institution of marriage.

Fortunately our bustling civilization has come to the rescue and declared that there shall be three stages in every relationship. The first is the courting, dating, or "seeing each other" stage. During which, couples are so logistically challenged that they do not have enough opportunities for sex to allow them to reach the threshold where one of them feels it is too often. The third stage is having children, from which point all bets are off.

Unfortunately that leaves the second, the dreaded "living together but no kids yet" stage, during which there are entirely too many opportunities to have sex, and as a result it is possible for one member of the couple to reach what a friend of mine once called the state of being "sufficiently suffonified."[1]

At this point a sort of Law of Supply And Demand may kick in, and it's different for the two sexes. When the female supply

---

1. D.G. Reid said this somewhere in Muskoka, Canada.

wants to be less than the male demand, and the difference isn't too great, the male will not lose interest or enthusiasm, and the female will have the choice of generously bestowing more than she herself needs, or drawing the line and still not losing any face. But things are not so rosy when the male supply is less than the female demand. The female may find the male to be inadequate, and the male is quite likely to see himself the same way: Indeed, because of the male's greater risk of performance anxiety, he may become capable of even less than he himself actually wants.

A man and a woman can find their way, if they are truly comfortable in each other's arms.

So maybe it's better the way nature designed it, with men the ones who are likely to want more sex during the "living together without children" years. That is, if that's even true. Some experts say that in terms of *hormonal levels*— which would seem to have a lot to do with desire—men and women both reach their peaks during their late teens or early twenties. It's just that the path to orgasm for men is a slam dunk, while for women it may be a longer dribble down the court. Once a woman finds her peak, though, she will probably not experience the same steady decline in fuel level that most men undergo over the years. (Enter Viagra and other "dysfunction"-curing drugs.)

What does all this come to, in terms of compatibility? Well, it seems at the very least that the issue of frequency may raise opportunities for negotiation for a couple. You and your partner will have times when you need to be able to gauge the other person's desire level, and care about it, so there will be no trouble. If you find you have friction, so to speak, with a man over this issue, you may want to stand back and ask yourself, is this really about frequency or is it about *intimacy*? When a man and a woman have loving intimacy, each one is going to know in an instant if the other is not fully engaged, and is not going to try for (or want) a solo flight.

And maybe that is the bottom line here. Maybe, in spite of nature's devious tricks, a man and a woman *can* find their way, if they are truly comfortable in each other's arms.

And that suggests one more factor in sexual compatibility.

The Seventh Factor...

What about *love*? Does being in love make two people more sexually compatible?

Well, we've just seen one good reason in favour of that claim. And when you think about it, most of the tricky ledges, curves, and grades that the choo-choo train of sex has to negotiate, are going to be easier when two people love each other.

They can work it out.

On the other hand, my mother once told me: It is better that the sex should be strong enough on its own to reignite the love when its flame is low.

BODY ISSUES

Dubious Norms that Shouldn't Rule

*W*hen I looked into the scientific and not-so-scientific literature on men's and women's body images, I was struck by two things.

First, there are a lot of different norms floating around, claiming to be the perceived male ideal for the female body in today's world. Let's look at some of them.

At one extreme we have the one for which the fashion industry is usually held responsible: As one writer put it, a woman's body is asked to look like that of "a tall, thin boy."[1] As a shape applied to women, this would have to be called *unnaturally* thin. Lots of literature links this norm to women's problems with body image and to anorexia.

Secondly, many scholarly articles refer to a "slim, athletic" ideal female body as being subscribed to by both men and women in contemporary Western culture, though scholarly research also indicates that African-American women are less worried about being thin and that they are supported by African-American men in this attitude.

---

1. From an online discussion called Debate Unlimited, by England's Martin Willett, found at http://mwillett.org/mind/bigwomen.htm. If you want to read a really eloquent, edgy, hilarious diatribe on this subject give it a look.

Then we have the image of some popular film and TV actresses (and glamour models), which has been referred to as "the curvaceously thin woman."[2] Harrison's article indicates that almost all women tend to think their breasts are either too small or too big to conform to this elusive standard.

Interestingly, the real world is in marked contrast to these images of thinness. A "SizeUSA" National Sizing Survey in 2004 indicated that men and women are both getting larger than they used to be, and that the average size of actual women is a twelve (this includes a full age range). The advantages for the weight-loss industry of the "norm" contrasted with the actual facts is all too apparent.

But even as an ideal, the School of Thin has competition. We find the "full-figured woman" making a surprise appearance as men's "resounding" favourite in an agitprop survey for Modestyle.com, in which men were asked what female figure they found most attractive. Full-figured (forty-five percent) easily won out over athletic (thirty-five percent) and very slim (twenty-four percent).

An August, 2004 survey by *Cosmopolitan* magazine offers a slightly different perspective that reminds us how much depends on how the choices are worded. Forced to choose among "svelte with big breasts," "curvy with an average rack," and "model-thin and small-chested," a whopping sixty-two percent of men chose "curvy with an average rack," an encouraging finding in that it favours a body type that is more common in nature than the other two.

Perhaps the most sensible and reassuring survey that I read was a 1990 *Times Mirror* Body Image Survey, which found that both men and women overestimate the importance of

2 "Television viewers' ideal body proportions: The case of the curvaceously thin woman," Kristen Harrison. *Sex Roles*. New York: Mar 2003. Vol. 48, Iss. 5/6, p. 255-264.

their bodies (as opposed to their faces) in the other sex's perception of them, and also guess wrongly about what physical features the other sex finds most desirable. Men think that women are primarily attracted by their physique (general build, rear, or chest), but women reply that a man's eyes are most important, followed not very closely by his build, face (which should get some credit for the eyes), smile, and rear. And most women like clean-shaven men with short, dark hair. More than half of male college grads and affluent men think that women prefer tall men, but in fact most women prefer men of average height. And although women think that men prefer thin women, the study found that about the same number of men like women with "generous" figures as like thin women.

You don't need to fall in love with the majority, you just need to fall in love with one man.

Now let's stop and think for a moment. As a woman who likes to be well-informed, are you going to read this report and say to yourself, "Oh my god, I've been pursuing the wrong type of man! I am not following the norm, so I must not be *normal*. I thought I liked tall guys with long hair and moustaches, but I guess I was wrong." I don't think you're going to do that. Why should you go against your own natural inclinations? Although I said in the last paragraph that "most women" prefer men of average height, I deliberately neglected to mention that fully a third (thirty-four percent) of women like tall men best. If you are one of them, you are solidly represented in the population; but reports that only mention what *most women* prefer would never tell you that.

And this is the second thing that struck me when I looked at the literature on body image. Many of the studies tend to obsess on what *most people* prefer. People want a winner, whether they're talking about body type, music, or politics; all other groups tend to be shovelled under the rug. But that makes no sense, and it needlessly discourages a lot of people. If I am a tall man, I should take an interest in the fact that thirty-four percent of women like my height, and not worry about those who don't. Thirty-four percent of women is a lot of women!!

The bottom line is this. It doesn't matter whether your natural body type is the "one" desired by a majority of men—assuming that anyone knows what that type is, which seems anything but clear! You don't need to fall in love with the majority, you just need to fall in love with one man.

So find your audience. Look for the people who like you the way you are naturally built. (That is, assuming that you are healthy, reasonably fit, and would feel good about yourself if the culture didn't tell you not to.) The good news is, no matter what your body type is, there are thousands of men out there who are seeking—nay, craving—that type. It should go without saying, don't choose a man who finds your body unacceptable, who in fact prefers women who look a different way. You're just setting yourself up for abuse. By the same token, if you have strong body type preferences in men, go with them. If you only like lean bald men with lots of chest hair, don't choose someone whose opposite characteristics will forever bother you.

The bad news is, if you don't accept *yourself*—regardless of your body type—the men who seek you won't have a chance. It does a man no good to find a woman who in his eyes is a total goddess if she won't let him admire her because *she takes exception to his admiration.*

Yet we live in a society where many women (and increasingly, men) hate their own bodies and faces. Why is this? A lot of the blame has to be laid at the feet of the corporations who profit from these attitudes. And the most ridiculous thing about the corporate critique of women is that it doesn't grant a pass to anybody. Its goal is to convince every single woman (and increasingly, every man) that she needs fixing in oh-so-many ways, that she is nothing more than a collection of flaws. That way she will never stop buying products and procedures to fix those flaws.

I don't know about you, but when I watch the makeover shows on cable TV, I find two things: At least fifty percent of the time I prefer the way the victim looks *before* her makeover; and at least seventy-five percent of the time I find the victim more attractive than the members of her makeover team. Who *are* these pushy, graceless experts? Who elected them god? Do they realize they are just shills for profiteers?

At least fifty percent of the time I prefer the way the victim looks before her makeover; and at least seventy-five percent of the time I find the victim more attractive than the members of her makeover team.

And so we have thousands of women driven to actual mutilation of their bodies by the desire to be anything but what they are. Women with large breasts have them reduced; women with small breasts have them augmented; faces are injected and cut to conform them to some freakish standard; and the age at which women and men feel they have to have facial work keeps getting lower. As more and more celebrities of a certain age start to look slightly odd, our culture needs to stop encouraging them, so they don't end up like Michael and Joan.

Obviously I'm not saying, "Don't go changing even if you are unhappy with the way you are." Of course, any man, woman, or child who tries to get *healthier* and *more active* is to be praised. My point about body type is just this: If you are healthy and active, you don't need to *change your natural body type to something else* in order to be "acceptable." Plenty of men will take their cue from Billy Joel and like you just the way you are. So don't let the media persuade you that you need fixing, or that you should conform to some arbitrary standard.

"A boy should have goals," a friend of mine was once told by a girl who would later dump him. The next chapter takes a look at that area.

16

LIFE GOALS AND AGENDA

Cabinet Men, Debtors, and Tormented Artists

*W*hat do the two of you want out of life? Where are you going? Where do you want to be in five years? What role do you want your partner to play in this quest, and vice versa?

This area involves your job, finances, vacation dreams, material things. And family, including the desire to have children.

CAREERS, JOBS, AND MONEY

Some people have a job; others have careers. A job gets you a paycheck to support the part of your life that you care about— the part when you aren't at the job. A career is paid work that you get real fulfillment out of. Some would say a career is work you would do even if you were independently wealthy.

The Torrid Tale of a Cabinet Man and a Psychologist

Braxton started installing kitchen and bathroom cabinets in new houses when he was fresh out of high school in Montreal. Back then it was just a job. What he cared about were the nights and the weekends, when he could be a Lothario on the loose. But even so, on the job he couldn't help being smart and aggressive, and in a few years he was in the office, helping to manage the guys out on the road. He soon realized that his boss was ineffectual. Braxton saw that their supplier was ripping them off and that the installers were being unfairly charged for construction flaws caused by home builders. He talked a banker friend into seeing these things too, and he started his own cabinet installation concern. At this moment a job started turning into a career.

Braxton was a natural leader, a fearless entrepreneur, and best of all, he knew how to get advice from the best. So Braxton's company prospered and grew, in fact it exploded as the housing boom happened. Soon he had bought out a cabinet manufacturer and eliminated a second bunch of problems. By the time he was forty, Brack was a multi-millionaire with a huge estate near Kingston, an ex-wife, and three kids that he saw on alternate weekends. He had a girlfriend, but it didn't feel like it was going anywhere.

Gradually Sheila realized that even if they got married she would be a cabinet widow.

It was then that he ran into Sheila. He had dated her in high school. They had had a torrid affair the last summer before she went to college and disappeared from his life. Now she was back, also divorced, with one child in high school. Brack and Sheila fell in love all over again. The sex was still hot, but slower and better, and now they were two grown-ups with a lot more to share. Sheila was a psychologist with two degrees, working in the criminal justice system. She liked her job, but it wore her out and she wished she could get into something else, or maybe just spend more time with her son, who was starting college in two years.

So it looked perfect for them. They had it all, including more money than they could ever spend. Brack took her to the finest restaurants; violinists serenaded their table.

There was just one problem: Braxton's damn career, his baby. He couldn't put it down. It consumed him seven days a week. His ex-wife now owned a big piece of it, and he had to keep her at bay too—if he left even for a week she might make a move he didn't like. So Sheila and Brack dated, and dated. Gradually Sheila realized that even if they got married she would be a *cabinet widow*. She would never have to work again, but she would also never be able to share the fruits of her own hard-working years with her husband. Sheila had a vision of what "the good life" could mean. It was she and Brack together, entertaining friends, camping, and travelling. Brack said he felt the same way, but his behaviour said something else. He was never there. His ego, his spirit, his fighting heart—they were all fully invested in his business. He was having a torrid affair with the empire he had created. It was never going to end.

Then Sheila met a legal aid lawyer. Hardworking, but not so ambitious. Not rich. Not flashy. He may not have been half the man Braxton was. But he was five times the partner, and he shared Sheila's vision. He wanted the same things out of life. And so he got them, with her.

The moral of this story is clear. When you're considering partnering with a man, you need to ask: How big a part of his life do I need his job to be? How big a part is it? How much of the rest of his time do I want to share? And he needs to ask the same things about you. That's a good lesson, but there is more to say about jobs and finances. Let's take a look at some major points:

- When you are getting serious about a man, take a serious interest in how he earns a living. Does he have a good job? If not, does he have a plan that you can believe in? Or do you not care, as long as he hauls home some kind of paycheque?
- Is his job a career, and if so is it the kind of consuming passion that Braxton's was, and are you all right with that? Listen to what he says about his job, whether he seems to think there's a future in it. Does he look forward to going to work? Does he dread it? How does he feel about advancement: Does he think it's likely, and does he want it? I'm not saying there are any right answers to these questions. I am saying, make sure you feel good about his situation and his attitudes to it; and make sure he feels the same way about your work.
- Look at the direction things are *heading* in. Consider where things are likely to be in five or ten years: Is that going to work for you?
- Part of getting to know a new person is getting to know his finances. We are taught that it is rude to ask someone about money, but if you are going to merge your life with someone else's, you will find yourself in the same financial boat. If you don't want to spend your life bailing, you had better see how leaky that boat is. And how likely it is to stay above water: This raises the dreaded spectre of debt.

Debt: The Gift that Keeps on Taking

Shawn and Alyssa were perfect for each other. The first few times they were together, they were addle-brained just because of each other's physical presence. She was a slim redhead and he was a husky blond, they both loved the beach and rock music. The first time they spent the night together, they slept the whole night on a couch entwined in each other's arms like kittens, and never woke up—even though Shawn normally needed a lot of space in bed.

They worked for the same company, Shawn in sales and Alyssa in customer service. Alyssa made a solid living, nothing spectacular. Shawn's income was more unpredictable (he was on commission), but he had a lot of style and Alyssa, whose last boyfriend had been a slob, liked the way Shawn wore his clothes. They had a whirlwind courtship and moved in together after two months. Alyssa had some nice furniture, but it wasn't enough for the three-bedroom home they bought, so they went out and got more. Two of the bedrooms had walk-in closets and that was fortunate because it took one of them just to house Shawn's fabulous collection of designer suits.

Everything was great except that Alyssa stopped enjoying any outing that involved spending money.

The trouble began slowly. They hadn't even discussed finances until one day in the supermarket when they had a cart full of groceries and Alyssa casually said, "So what do we do, go halfies or take turns?" Shawn reacted as if it was an awkward topic, as if she had said something gauche. Then he perversely insisted on paying the whole bill, and they were both quiet on the way home.

But Alyssa brought it up again, and Shawn reluctantly admitted that it was a valid topic. So they agreed on a fifty-fifty split of mutual expenses. They would take turns paying for things—groceries, gas, and house bills—and keep track of who owed what. The only problem was that Shawn never seemed to think it was his turn. Alyssa kept a record of their expenses and that ledger book was very neat, but it never showed any contributions from Shawn.

Everything was great except that Alyssa stopped enjoying any outing that involved spending money—which includes a lot of outings. And Shawn loved to buy things, as long as he didn't have to use cash. Not just suits and shirts, he also salivated over audiophile speakers and high-definition TVs. And he didn't seem to be satisfied with their furniture yet. He craved a reclining chair with shiatsu massage and he needed the mattress with the sleep numbers. Alyssa wanted no part of such reckless spending. So either she went along and became a wet blanket, or she stayed home and couldn't rein in his spending. Neither did the credit card companies do anything to discourage him; they were too busy lobbying for a law that made bankruptcy almost impossible.

In less than a year Alyssa found herself supporting two people—two people who were no longer getting along so well. Her salary was barely adequate for such a load, and Shawn's take-home pay was now less than the minimum payments on his credit cards. So his debt became hers, and every month their net assets were less. The only way out of this mess was for Shawn to go through bankruptcy—but that was no longer a viable option. Less than two years after they moved in together, Shawn had changed in Alyssa's eyes from a financial equal to a dependent, and in his eyes she had become a scolding mother figure, a bad news bear.

Debt had sucked the magic right out of their relationship.

Now I am not saying avoid people who are in debt. If you did you'd have to avoid most of the population, these days. Minor debt is common and is not crippling, and even major debt can be dealt with, when it is faced squarely and honestly. Two people as a team can often defeat debt quicker than one person alone. What I am saying is, find out what you are getting into before you get into it, and decide whether you *want* to deal with it and if so, how you are *going* to deal with it. Face the financial music.

Chasing an Artistic Dream as a Career Choice

There is a kind of dream that tends to put any normal career path on hold: the dream of being an actor, a songwriter, a painter, a poet, or god forbid, a writer. The problem is, creative people often don't want to commit to any *serious* job, because they think it will pull them too far off their chosen track.

Take Chris, rock star wannabe. Even though he has a degree in history and could get his teaching certificate, Chris doesn't want to be a school teacher, because...well, if pressed he'll tell you it's because *songwriters don't teach school*. (Apparently Chris never heard of Gordon Sumner, who was a teacher at a Catholic girls' school in England before he hit it big as Sting, leader of The Police.)

Songwriters, Chris says, hang out in rock clubs and drink a lot of Jack Daniels and wear black and look very skinny and dangerous. Chris can't do something as respectable as teaching; he can't be bourgeois; he can't tie himself down to a long-term job because what if that big call comes from a record company—he has to be ready to hit the road, right?

If you're considering being Chris' mate, you may want to fast-forward a decade or two and contemplate the likely outcome of Chris' quest.

The odds are not good for creative people. In most careers, if you have ability and apply yourself, you will achieve a reasonable amount of success. Not so for artists—that is why they are called *tormented*. Sadly, most artists don't make it, talented or not. Most don't even get a chance: Their work isn't noticed by the increasingly timid corporate entities that could make them successful. Their work doesn't get published—the public never even gets to vote on whether it's any good. A few do get the big break, a few who are luckier than they will ever admit, and a small percentage of these actually achieve substantial sales and make it.

Back to Chris: His story may unfold this way. He will go on for years, eking out a living as a part-time waiter or courier or retail clerk. He will have some close calls, will almost get a record deal. But the woman who backed him at Ripoff Records will move to another career and the new A & R person won't be into Chris' blues-punk style.

So Chris won't ever have a real career. Why? Because he is waiting for the ship that will never come in. He won't do his number-two choice, school teaching, because he wants to do number one, being a rock star. But number one won't happen. So instead he'll end up doing choices number twenty-seven, twenty-eight, and twenty-nine. Jobs he isn't into, that don't earn enough money to afford him much of a life.

If Chris could somehow jump ahead two decades, if he could look back from that future vantage point and see how those years will be squandered, you know he would not choose jobs twenty-seven, twenty-eight, and twenty-nine. He would knuckle under and do job number two, an actual career. And then he might even have enough money to invest in his own songwriting.

But Chris can't see ahead, can't see that it won't happen for him. He refuses to admit that possibility. And there is always the chance that he's right, that his dream *will* come true, if he is very hardworking and has the promotional chip in his brain as well as the creative one.

In fact there is something heroic about creative people, who put their lives on hold to pursue a dream. I'm not saying don't choose one as your mate; and if you are one, I'm not saying you're not a worthy mate. I'm just saying go into this kind of life with your eyes open, and go into it because you and your partner share those values. Go into it knowing that the only rewards may be the romance of a true heart's quest, and the precious things an artist creates. Have a backup plan for income. Prepare to be entertained, and prepare for a bumpy ride!

Here are a few questions to ask if you are considering hitching your wagon to a struggling artist. They will help you assess his chances. It all comes down to this: Is he taking the risks, and is he doing the work?

1. Is he exposing his work to his peers and to the public? Artists who later make it first put their stuff out there and test it, and they usually get good reactions from other artists and from the public.
2. Does he take advantage of every opportunity, especially for promotion and networking? Some artists—including some of the best ones—love the creation part, they write, paint, compose prolifically, but when it comes to selling themselves they back off. They don't network, they don't make appointments with the industry, they don't risk rejection. But I have seen artists who are not the most talented do well, because they know how to cultivate contacts and get bookings.

3. If the answer to number 2 was no, then the question becomes, does he have someone to do the selling *for* him? Most creative people need someone to represent them: Writers need an agent, songwriters need a publisher, and so on. But on the way up, most artists have to act as their own agent, if only to build up enough of a track record to get a professional to represent them. If your tormented genius doesn't want to sell himself, he had better have someone to represent him.

4. Finally, are you the missing piece? Some artists are lucky enough to find a partner who can supply what they cannot: expertise at promotion, Web site design, and booking. If you know how to do these things, you are likely to have a real-world perspective on an artist's chances; and if you choose to sign on with him, you are likely to have your eyes wide open. For a couple to pursue a single dream together is an intense journey, fraught with pitfalls, but it has been known to succeed, more than once.

It all comes down to working hard and taking risks. People who do these two things are likely to get to a definite verdict: "I can make it at this, or I can't." It's fun to be with someone who really tries. Even if they fail, they had the glory of bravely fighting for a goal. If the dream won't come true, they are likely to realize it in time and do something else.

DESIRE FOR CHILDREN

It hardly needs saying that a couple had better agree on whether they want kids. This is one point on which you want to be *alike*.

If you both honestly don't want to have kids, that can work out okay. There can be lots of legitimate reasons for this.

Maybe you're too into your careers, and are honest enough to admit it. Maybe you met too late in life. Maybe you already have enough kids; you've cheerfully given your best to them, and you are ready to move on.

If you both want kids, that is an important point of agreement. But it doesn't prove you are right for each other. In fact it just raises the stakes of compatibility in every other area. For example, religion. A childless couple may be able to finesse the fact that he is a devout Catholic and she is an atheist (though it won't be easy!). But when it comes time to raise children, they are going to have two contradictory views of what the child should be taught. That can quickly become a deal breaker in a marriage.

As we all know, raising children is an exhausting, frenetic, issue-laden enterprise. It involves split-second decisions and it requires nerves of steel, a backbone of granite, and laser eyes. Not to mention patience and hard work. Child rearing will expose the fault lines in a couple quicker than anything else.

Raising children requires nerves of steel, a backbone of granite, and laser eyes.

If one of you already has kids, the issue is no longer hypothetical. Real little people are involved. If the one with kids wants a co-parent, that will have to be talked and tested out, in a gradual way that is fair to all parties. By the way, if you are a single or divorced mom, the Internet can be a big help to you in finding men who are more than open to a woman with kids. As we'll see in Part Three, you can filter in advance for attitude to children. For example, there are men out there who missed the children boat and who may feel it's too late to start a family, but would welcome a chance to join one in progress. And you can find them.

Then there is the toughest case: A couple who *don't know* if they want to have kids. Maybe they're in their twenties, are just launching careers and it just isn't an issue yet. But eventually it will be an issue. One of them will come up with a definite answer to the children question, and the other had better agree. If the verdict is yes, one of them may have to compromise career goals—and they had better know which one.

We live in a world where children have a whole host of problems that they didn't use to have—medical, emotional, and cognitive. Diseases that were hardly heard of a couple of generations ago are rampant: Thousands of kids are being treated with powerful drugs for ADD, asthma, and other disorders. Thoughtful couples are trying to deal with the fact that, as Dr. Laura says, children are not pets. You shouldn't "acquire" them if you don't really want (or simply don't have time) to parent them. If children are consigned to nannies and daycare and TV, if they live separate lives in households where everyone has their own virtual universe (TV and computer) in their own rooms, they are more likely to go astray. Only active parenting can rectify this.

So if you have met a man who you think may be Mr. Right, you need to talk about this. You need to explore each other's feelings and goals around having and raising kids. The single most helpful factor here may be *family of origin as a role model*. If you and your new love find common ground in the homes you came from, and the ways you were raised as children, you have a very strong foundation to build on. This common ground can even be negative: Maybe you both don't like the way you were raised, and you agree on how you want to do better.

SUPPORTING EACH OTHER'S ACHIEVEMENTS

Sometimes one spouse is high profile and gets a lot of public attention and praise, and the other labours less visibly. Even then there needs to be a balance between the two people, in terms of appreciating each other's efforts in life. (If one person is the wind beneath the other's wings, that support had better be cherished and celebrated.) In most cases people have some separate goals, and some shared ones. Partners should be highly interested in each other's struggles and strivings. They should want to hear about them and want to help, when help is asked for.

Whether your job or hobby is a big deal or not, whether his is, you should be his biggest fan.

And he should be your biggest fan.

So take note, when you're getting to know a man, as to whether you both seem to take time to care about the other one's quests.

CULTURE

Not Excluding Sports, TV, and Pets

*C*ulture starts with work. How you support yourself is a big part of your personal culture. Especially if you have a career that you worked hard for. A doctor has made a commitment to Western science that already places her at a certain cultural vantage point. A clothing designer will have a set of highly developed perceptions and passions that are unique. A baseball player has fallen in love with a whole tradition of effort, achievement, and record-keeping. A corporate executive likewise has bought into a package of values that lots of people don't share. If you or your prospective mate has an intense career like these, make sure that it doesn't constitute a wall between you. I'm certainly not advocating that mates have the same career, but the same general path (e.g., business, sports, the arts) can be a very good thing, because it gives you so much to talk about, and it makes it more likely that you won't have conflicting values. If you could never abide your children hanging out on the weekend in the hall of a law firm, don't marry a lawyer.

When all the work is done, we're left with the things we like to do to entertain ourselves. These may seem like luxuries, but from a relationship point of view they are not. They may be the most important things you need to have in common with your mate. Work can be a great way of bonding, but even when their careers are similar, most couples don't work together; even parents usually divide labour.

So your best chance to hang on to the bond you had when you were dating is to enjoy doing things together in your spare time. Let's take a few examples.

SPECTATOR SPORTS

According to one theory, what we do instead of killing each other is, we watch sports. Sports events provide a harmless way to work off a lot of the aggression that is hard-wired into our species, the deep need males especially have, to best someone else physically. It's also a safer place to put patriotic aggression (i.e., the desire to prove that one's own country is better than everyone else's by vanquishing the others in battle).

In any case, the world is divided into those who take sports very seriously, and those who don't. For a lot of men (and some women), leisure time is utterly dominated by the need to monitor their teams of choice (or in some cases, all the teams in the league). Far from being optional, these hours feel like a religious devotion. And it's true that sharing the excitement, suspense, fine points, and outcome of a good game is a pretty cool way of bonding with other people.

Again it comes down to what works for you. Some couples love to watch tennis together; some love the NFL; and some see the game as a male preserve, a time when the guys gather in front of the TV and the women do "other things" that somehow result in the men eating. When you're getting to know a man, check out his agenda in this area, observe how much it matters to him, and see how that fits you.

PARTICIPANT SPORTS

One of the sad losses of adulthood is that people feel they can no longer do the things they used to do as kids—unless they are really good at them. When you're a kid you get to play sports even if you aren't that good, and you get the amazing outlet of trying to hit a ball or shoot a puck. You get to leave the verbal part of your brain behind and use the physical co-ordination that is one of the joys of being alive. But then you are older and suddenly it isn't okay to be anything less than professional. Life doesn't pick you for its team anymore.

When you get older, life doesn't pick you for its team anymore.

Some people don't let this stop them. They get their own games together, they insist on having some physical fun. They don't obsess on winning, and they honour everyone's chance to play at their own skill level. This can be a wonderful break from the rat race, it can free people from the roles they have to play at work, and it can help a couple bond with a wider group. If you are this way inclined, check out your prospective mate's feelings in this area.

Then we have the Intrepid Family. Terry was an active woman of thirty who taught computer science at a community college. She jogged regularly and worked out. She also liked to read books. When she met Nick at a party, she liked his bright energy and his enthusiasm for his job in physical therapy. What she wasn't ready for was what came with him as a package deal. Turned out that Nick liked to spend a whole lot of his leisure time with his family of origin, and they liked to spend all their time outdoing each other at physical feats. The Intrepid Family were a strenuously fun group, full of noise and laughter. They snow-skied, they water-skied, they played tennis, baseball, touch football; they climbed, they camped, they fished, they dove, they swam, and they sailed. They were always daring each other to try harder and take greater risks. Only one thing scared them: Show them a Henry James novel and their tans would drain of colour.

Terry found that she had two choices: Get caught up in the Intrepid Family activities, or say *ciao* to Nick. She chose to leave 'em instead of joining 'em: It was the only way to save her own spare hours for the things she loved to do.

THE ARTS

Some people approach the arts with the same fervour often applied to sports. She who does is unlikely to fit well with a partner who is indifferent to the music, TV shows, films, books, or paintings that make her world go round. So it pays to ask yourself some of these questions about how you and your possible mate relate to the arts:

- How picky are you? Do you like pretty much whatever is popular, or do you divide what's out there into a lot that you hate, and a few that you love? Does your world revolve around certain nights of the week because that's when your favourite show is on, or are you content to watch whatever's on? Is he like you? Degree of pickiness is a good index to compatibility.
- Do you and he like a lot of the same things? Does he love glam rock and it just grates on you? Do you hate horror

movies and he finds them delicious? Do you read much, and if so can you talk to him about books?

- Do you like analyzing movies, TV shows, other arts? For those who do, this is an almost limitless source of entertaining and highly personal conversation that can make two people feel incredibly close; for those who don't, it can be a royal pain.

Come to think of it, these three questions apply equally well to spectator sports, the appreciation of which can give just as much pleasure to two people who see eye to eye about them.

Do you like sitcoms? Do you like prime time TV? Do you like the football game blaring? Do you like the TV on when no one is watching? Do you like TV at all? Can you stand it if the remote is in somebody else's hands? Can you do something else while the TV is on?

You and your man are going to create your new world: TV habits may be a very large part of that world. Will you like living there?

EDUCATION, INTELLECT (AND INTELLIGENCE)

Education and intellect aren't the same thing. Lots of people who don't have advanced degrees are deep thinkers, and lots of people with Ph.D.s are not. I don't think you need to be an expert in the same areas that your partner is, I don't even think you need to read the same books. But you had better be interested (and competent) listeners to each other's intellectual reports. This is particularly true when one is not a professional in one's area of intellectual interest. A professional is safe in the arms of her peers: A professor of cultural anthropology has her academic colleagues to turn to for feedback and stimulation, and they are more than capable of appreciating her best thoughts on the subject. But someone who didn't get a job related to their advanced degree may be more isolated, and may crave more intellectual feedback from their partner. Do you feel your best thoughts are appreciated by your partner?

Degree of pickiness is a good index to compatibility. If you are an analytical person you are going to be better off with a mate who is too. I know a couple—know them very well—whose favourite activity is debriefing each other after an evening out with friends. When they have to attend an event in separate cars that is a huge problem for them, because they like to tell each other in novelistic detail about all the juicy encounters they had that evening, and then they like to analyze those encounters: It is their dear hobby. To have to wait till they get home to begin this entertainment is just too hard.

Speaking of intelligence (which I was supposed to do), it comes in several varieties. You can be very smart in one area and pretty dumb in another, and happy couples are often strong in different areas. There is the ability to grasp facts, which comes in very handy at a lot of jobs and while watching (or writing) mystery stories. There is logical skill, a talent for detecting contradictions and formulating thoughts in a way that "says it exactly"—very useful in someone whose job is putting legislation together, or teaching academic philosophy. There is mathematical prowess—which often goes with logic. There is musical talent. Visual/artistic talent. There is psychological acumen; scientific imagination...and there are many other areas of intelligence.

Some of these areas emerge in ordinary conversation: They show themselves in the form of wit, humour, originality, cogency, the ability to formulate or follow a complex thought. People are pretty good at detecting intelligence (or its lack) in others, and it is highly advisable to choose a partner who can meet you on a level playing field, at least regarding the topics you want to share. It is also advantageous to choose a partner whose mind balances yours, by having different areas of greatest strength. That way one person can make sure the taxes are right while the other can explain the plot of *Law and Order*.

ANIMALS AND PETS

We have dog people, cat people, and people whose five pets sleep with them in their bed. When you take on a partner, you're taking on everyone that partner sleeps with.

And now, one more chapter on compatibility: it concerns the crucial area of values.

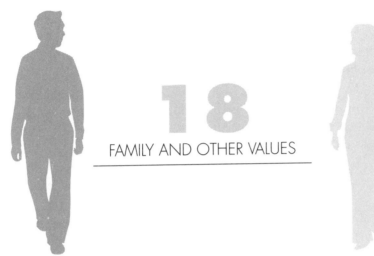

18

FAMILY AND OTHER VALUES

FAMILY-OF-ORIGIN

We are programmed much more than we may admit by the family we grew up in. It functions as a role model both in its positive and its negative features, and it creates expectations of what "normal" means. Your sense of what a family can be, owes a lot to the family you came from. What you are comfortable with in terms of income, lifestyle, and emotional atmosphere is heavily influenced by your family of origin. All families are dysfunctional to some extent, but if your family gave you a picture of basic stability and love, you carry that as an ideal into your romantic relationships. It helps enormously if your partner does too.

One of the biggest losses many people sustain is that of the family they once had. For such people, that family was a safe, nurturing place, where good times happened, close bonds existed, and death was a distant dream. When you grow up and leave that behind (especially if you end up moving away), there is a grief and sadness that you carry around for years, a feeling of having no home. Then you meet someone and all at once it seems as if those things you lost, you can have again with this person.

Part of what happens when we fall in love is that we feel we are coming home again. Suddenly it seems possible to create a family to replace the one we lost, whether it's with children or not.

Part of what happens when we fall in love is that we feel we are coming home again.

I'm not saying that we are all pre-destined to repeat what our family was. I'm saying, pay a lot of atten-tion to your prospective partner's family of origin, to what he says about them, whether he recalls them fondly, how he relates to them now. If he repudiates them, look into that and learn from it. These things are a window on the home he will cre-ate with you.

VALUES

In recent decades, politics, religion, and values in gener-al have been heated up to the point where it is harder and harder to be tolerant of opposing views. The political media have been taken over by highly funded armies whose main purpose is to confuse, frighten, and polarize the audience. The main casualty is truth, which is now too expensive and too controversial for so-called news organizations to pursue. Instead, in the name of phony "balance," every claim, no matter how favoured by the evidence, is pestered by an op-posite claim. Those statements backed by the most corporate money tend to win.

Winning has consequences. It determines whether young men and women go to foreign countries and die, whether a woman can have an abortion, whether gay couples can get married. It determines who gets lower taxes and whether social security and Medicare will survive. It determines what is taught to children.

In this atmosphere it is pretty hard to be neutral. The consequences of people's beliefs are so dire that it even gets hard not to hate those who disagree with you. Take religious beliefs for example. Maybe half a century ago they used to seem like something nice that folks talked about on Sunday and didn't worry much about the rest of the time. Now they don't seem so warm and fuzzy, since the Twin Towers came down and the Christian Right took a tight grip on the Republican Party in the US. It isn't so easy anymore to say it doesn't matter what someone thinks about religion. And politics: It may be just a game, but it's a game played for high stakes, from soldiers' lives to the question of whether the planet will continue to extend its hospitality to human beings.

If you plan to have children the issues become even more inescapable, because someone has to decide what your children are going to be taught.

If you and your partner disagree on fundamental values, good luck. So you had better find out whether you do.

POLITICS

Allegiance to a party or a cause tends to be more rabid, the less it is supported by thought and fact. Unexamined loyalty is not always a good thing. Unfortunately we live in a time when a lot of people get their political views like fast food: already cooked, backed by a lot of hype, and of dubious origin. The views being sold on TV and talk radio are extreme: Pundits on the right and the left revile each other, and encourage their listeners to do the same. Seems everyone is a witch hunter these days. It's gotten to the point where both sides—liberals and conservatives—call the other murderers. (Accusations based on war and abortion.)

If you and your prospective partner both prefer to be apolitical, that may avert problems. If one of you cares about politics and the other doesn't, that is less likely to fly. *Not caring is a position that someone else can be in conflict with.*

Let's say you both are political. Then you had best try talking about political issues. If you generally fall on the same side, that'll work. If you don't, then watch for the rabidity that I mentioned a moment ago. Watch for positions that are shrill, aggressive, and can't abide questioning. They are unlikely to be able to bear disagreement. See whether the two of you are able to sift a topic in a rational way, to give calm reasons for your views. See if you are each able to acknowledge some truth in the opposing view. If so, a liberal may be able to be in a relationship with a conservative, they may even have a good time sparring about their issues, and they may in time educate each other and forge a third philosophy that is less rigid.

A lot of people get their political views like fast food: already cooked, backed by a lot of hype, and of dubious origin.

Along those lines, you can maximize your potential for compatibility with someone in another political camp if you *separate one issue from another.* Maybe the worst thing about today's feud between the left and the right is that it sweeps issues together that would be better kept separate, and forces an all-or-nothing response. If you like the right-wing pundits, you are supposed to follow them down *every* road. Their argument goes like this: "You're against legalized abortion, right? Liberals favour it. All right then, you have to oppose *everything* the liberals believe. They are against the war in Iraq. So you have to be for it. They believe global warming is a serious threat to our survival. So you have to scoff at it."

This leaves no room for looking at each issue on its own merits. No room to be against legalized abortion and acknowledge that the war in Iraq might be a mistake, or that global warming might be about to flood the world's coastlines. If you find yourself in a bad place when talking politics with your date, try separating the issues.

ORGANIZED RELIGION

A good way to focus the issue of organized religion, is to ask yourself, do you (or would you) want your children to be indoctrinated into the dogmas of a particular religion?

There are a lot of different answers floating around.

Some people don't think of religion as a set of beliefs to be signed onto, but more as a branch of literature. They may still want their children to be taught *comparative religion*, to better understand world history and current events. They may describe themselves as "spiritual but not religious," or as agnostics or atheists. In the eyes of organized religion they are non-believers.

Some people are faithful and devout churchgoers, who are likely to want their children inducted into the very denomination they are members of.

And in the middle are a whole lot of people who are slightly vague about religion. Their main reason for belonging to a given religious organization may be cultural rather than religious: Jews who want their children to have a Bar/Bat Mitzvah; Christians who enjoy the carols and candles at Christmastime; people of any stripe who want a religious wedding. But most of the time these quasi-religious folks don't attend services, and unless they are politicians, they don't talk a lot about god. Interestingly, according to a study in *The Christian Century*, these people report to pollsters that they attend church more often than they actually do. Even in the US, which has higher service attendance than Canada or England, twice as many people claim to be regular churchgoers as actually are.

People in this middle group are believers of a sort, but what exactly they believe may vary a lot. They may have a buffet approach to organized religion, accepting the parts of it that seem useful and ignoring the rest.

Most of the time these quasi-religious folks don't attend services, and unless they are politicians, they don't talk a lot about god.

I think the "what do you want your children taught" question can go a long way towards smoking out the truth about what people believe, how strongly they believe it, and whether there is serious disagreement within a couple. Devout believers obviously could have a problem partnering with non-believers. But when one member of the couple is in the middle (quasi-religious) group, there can also be issues. The middle view is a position too, and it can fail to satisfy someone at either end of the spectrum.

Even when both partners are in the middle group, issues could be waiting. Behind a lagging churchgoer may lurk a gung-ho believer waiting to redeem himself—or a non-believer waiting to make the final break—and what better occasion to do this than on the advent of children?

So talk to your new beau about this. Make it hypothetical, approach it with a light touch if you will, but talk about it, and see where the talk leads.

That concludes my look at some colourful (and sometimes neglected) facets of compatibility. Now that we've sharpened up the tools for recognizing whether a man is right for you, you may well wish you had more men to apply them to. That is what Part Three is all about: the huge opportunity that is online dating.

PART

FINDING MR. RIGHT ONLINE

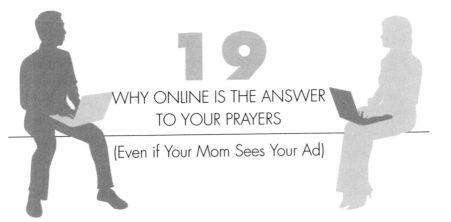

19

WHY ONLINE IS THE ANSWER TO YOUR PRAYERS

(Even if Your Mom Sees Your Ad)

*I*n Part One I talked about some of the good venues in which to encounter a man and begin to know him. The problem is quantity. The more candidates you get a look at, the better your odds of finding a suitable partner. How many men do you get a chance to meet in these ways? How many private parties do you get invited to, how many men do you manage to talk to in Desirable Bars? It seems that the most I can advise you to do regarding most of these settings is to go to them when possible, and be prepared, be open, be alert to opportunities—*if* they materialize. This advice does work, and these venues alone have allowed many women to find a good mate. But they don't always provide enough grist for the sighting mill.

The good news is, there is one venue that can fix the odds, that can throw so many good chances your way that you will literally not have time to field them all (unless you have the time-saving tips of a book like this).

It's a new venue: It didn't even exist until the last decade of the twentieth century. It has changed the world, and it has changed the world of mating. For the first time in human history, you can sit in the comfort, safety, and privacy of your own home and you can cast a net over the whole planet. Think of it, men *are* out there who are right for you. (In the past it seemed like they weren't, but wasn't that just because they were so hard to find?) Some may be in your city, some may be far away. In the past you had no way of encountering them, unless they happened to walk into the room—and how likely was that?

But now you do. And men do. Millions of people are now reporting for romantic duty.

THE "YOU" CLUB

Let's do what the philosophers call a "thought experiment." Theirs tend to involve quantum cats and clever zombies, but ours will involve men. One of the problems of meeting people in the real world is that it takes a long time to get to know them, and you may discover deal breakers way down the line. If only there were a way to know more about someone in *advance...*

Now imagine for a moment that you can go to a gathering every week, and there are lots of single men there, and *all* of them

- Are in the age range that you would want;
- Are the right height and body type to suit you;
- Live in your area;
- Have income you deem acceptable;
- Share your approaches to drinking and smoking;

- Have a political leaning you are comfortable with;
- Agree with you about whether to have children or are cool with children you already have;
- Have the same religious affiliation or lack thereof as you...

...and so on. In addition these men have all passed the "Prose Test." They have submitted a charming little essay to you, in which they used their own words to express who they are, what they value, and who they're looking for. You did the same for them, and both sides liked what they read.

Now imagine that you look the group over and narrow it down to the men you find physically attractive, and then make sure that you are noticed by each of these, and strike up a conversation with the ones you seem to click with...

Would that be worth doing?

Well, guess what: We just ran through a standard search on a good dating site.

The "You" Club is meeting; do you think you might want to attend?

Think about this for a moment. Using multiple choice questions and personal pieces that you write, you can list the characteristics you seek in a man—mental, physical, emotional, whatever—and you can describe yourself. And then you can wait while millions of men consider what you have said. And whenever one of them decides that he may indeed be what you are seeking, and vice versa, you can have the adventure of contact: an e-mail or Instant Message from him. You control which men contact you, by the profile you offer. Imagine hearing only from men who like that profile.

But of course, you don't have to wait. You can choose to be more aggressive. You can voyage through the words and photos men have used to present themselves, and you can find men who seem to be right for you, and you can contact them. In a way, this is a more cautious approach, because it lets you keep control of information until contact is made, lets you be reticent about yourself until you have found a target.

Either way, you may as well get used to one thing:

It is actually possible, even *probable*, that if you make a decent effort in Internet dating, you can find a splendid lifetime partner online.

To help you achieve exactly that, I will provide an in-depth, detailed guide to finding Mr. Right online. What I talked about in Parts One and Two will come in very handy now, for the reason I gave in the Introduction: once you meet a desirable guy, the fact that you found him online matters much less than what goes on in person.

Among my topics are

- Dating sites: features you need
- Look before you pay: the joys of free searching
- A good photo set: what to shoot for
- How to create a winning online ad
- A portrait of three top sites
- Matchmaking sites: the curious case of eHarmony.com
- How to eliminate Mr. Wrongs
- What happens if you find Mr. Right and he isn't local? Are long-distance relationships worth bothering with?
- How to conduct an Internet romance: why you should avoid falling in love before you meet in person
- The first in-person meeting: what to wear, what to ask, what to watch for and watch *out* for.

MYTH-BUSTING 201:
COMMON MISCONCEPTIONS ABOUT ONLINE DATING

Before we begin our detailed exploration of the online dating process, let's revisit the myths from Chapter 7, the ones that discouraged women from going to a bar alone. I said that these myths would crop up again in connection with looking for a mate online. Let's see how they look in this context.

Myth No. 1: Men Online Only Want One Thing.

Given that millions of men are online looking, it stands to reason that some of them are going to be looking for the fast track to sex. Probably about the same percentage who are looking for that in the real world. The thing is, the Internet dating world has come a long way since its inception in the 1990s: It has developed sites that cater to every conceivable market, and these sites *make more money if they make their purposes clear.*

In addition these men have all passed the "Prose Test." They have submitted a charming little essay to you, and you liked it.

There are lots of sites dedicated to sexual encounters: sites like AdultFriendfinder.com and the "Intimate Encounters" section of Lavalife.com. These sites are full of ads from men and women who are looking to hook up without a lot of strings attached.

There are also many sites clearly dedicated to dating and long-term relationships, like Match.com and the "Dating" and "Relationship" sections of Lavalife. There are sites like eHarmony whose only purpose is to bring about happy marriages.

Now if you were a man looking for sex, where would you go? Sites cost money. You're not going to spend it on one that isn't offering what you want.

That leaves the millions of men who have chosen to pay for membership on dating and relationship sites. It doesn't take a rocket scientist to see that they are looking for dating and relationships.

Myth No. 2: Only Sluts Look for Men Online. Or, If I Put an Ad on a Dating Site, I'll Look Like a Slut.

I guess we've answered this one. See myth 1.

Myth No. 3: A Woman Cannot Call the Shots Online; It Is a Male Stronghold.

This myth doesn't really translate into the online context: It's worth looking at just to savour that pleasant fact.

If there was ever a level playing field, the modern dating site is it. It's level in the sense that users call the shots of their own experiences. You control how you present yourself, and with whom you interact.

You can contact any man you want to, by sending a gentle feeler (sometimes called a "wink") or an e-mail. You don't have to put up with nuisance men: You can block their e-mails, and you can take steps not to attract them in the first place. When a desirable man contacts you, you control how much access he gets to you.

You are in charge.

Myth No. 4: A Woman Who Goes on a Dating Site Looks Like She Is *Desperate* for Love.

Well, if that's true, then millions of women are looking like they are desperate for love. It doesn't seem to be hurting their chances.

As I said in the Introduction, online dating has long since reached a tipping point: When enough people do something, it becomes normal, accepted. If you're the only lone woman in a bar, you can at least wonder how that might be misinterpreted (by Mr. Wrongs). But there is absolutely no chance that you are going to be the only lone woman on a dating site: They're all flying solo, and there are thousands of them. The women on a dating site are in exactly the same situation as the men. Your presence there will appear crashingly normal.

Myth No. 5: Serious Relationships Never Begin Online.

I, for one, disagree. So does my spouse, who found me on AOL.

As one engaged couple put it, when you meet this way "you get to know people from the inside out."

And we are not a fluke. Most of the good dating sites have a Success Stories section, where you can read hundreds of tales of happy couples who met on that site, written by the couples themselves. According to Match.com, every year over 200,000 of their users find love. eHarmony says that it is responsible for more than 16,000 marriages a year. Several studies report that couples who met online are more optimistic, more satisfied, and more in love than those who didn't.

The reason for that may be the one I gave earlier: they had more of a choice. According to an oft-quoted Pew Survey of online dating (March 5, 2006), one of the main reasons why people use online dating sites is that they believe that "online dating helps people find a better match because they have access to a larger pool of potential dates."

There's another reason too. By reading a person's profile and exchanging e-mails, you find out a whole lot about them that might take months or years to know in the old-fashioned world. You don't have the magic of their physical presence to distract you from the treasures of conversation. By e-mail and then later by telephone, *you learn to talk and listen to each other*. You learn to enjoy each other's minds. You get good at that or you don't go on. As one engaged couple put it, when you meet this way "you get to know people from the inside out."

The bottom line: People are looking for love online because they think it's a better way to find love that lasts.

Myth No. 6: Meeting Men Online Is Not Safe.

Well, let's see.

Online you can get to know a man and decide whether you are interested in him without revealing your identity or being in the same room with him.

You can Instant Message (IM) and e-mail to your heart's content through the site's anonymous network, so your own personal IM and e-mail are not known to your new friend until you are good and ready to share them, if ever. That is because the smart people who developed online dating realized that customers wouldn't go for it unless they could protect their anonymity. So they went to great lengths to make that happen.

Later I offer safety tips such as when and where to meet in person for the first time, and what personal information to protect until you are sure of someone. The major dating sites also have safety pages that will help and reassure you.

Yes, there are con artists and predators out there, just as there are when you encounter people in the real world. It's good to exercise some common sense, follow safety guidelines, use the anonymity that the good sites offer, and above all, use your own good judgment about people—your own finely tuned ability to detect a phony.

Finally, there is safety in numbers. As more and more people flock to the adventure, it gets safer.

Having said all this, there is still some nagging residue of resistance that lurks in all of us. It might be put as follows:

PROBLEM: I'M IN TROUBLE IF MY MOTHER SEES MY AD

Oh god, my personal ad will be visible online! What if my mom sees it? Or my co-worker; or my ex?

Well, take comfort in this: It's kind of like catching someone with their eyes open during a prayer. If your mom sees it, it's probably because she is trolling for love on the same site. This might not be too much of a stretch: According to Yahoo! Personals, baby boomers (now aged forty-seven to sixty-one) are seeing their kids succeed at online dating, and can't resist joining the fun. Match.com reports that boomers are its quickest growing segment, approaching two million.

The other thing is, if your mom sees your ad, she is probably gay—I hope you knew that.

The best revenge against friends or family members who spy your ad, is finding theirs.

OVERVIEW OF THE PROCESS

Scanning, Signing Up, and Subscribing

$\mathcal{I}$n today's Internet dating world you can find major sites, minor sites, niche sites for every possible persuasion, free sites of various types, and whatever else the busy Web entrepreneurs have come up with lately. I will touch on most of these, but will mainly discuss the paid sites, because they offer the most full-featured experience, the most potent resources, and the most committed users. In particular I will draw portraits of three of the top dating sites in the world—Match.com, Yahoo! Personals, and Lavalife—and of the major matchmaking site, eHarmony.com. These four sites all have interesting and unique features; by looking at them, you'll get a good picture of what features you do and don't care about, and what features you may want to look for on other sites.

The process of engaging with a paid dating site has three steps:

- Scanning
- Signing up
- Subscribing

Only the last step involves money coming out of your pocket.

Scanning means looking around a site without identifying yourself in any way.

Signing up means choosing a username and password, providing an e-mail address, creating a profile (the information you'll be known by on the site), and providing a photo or set of photos. Signing up doesn't cost anything.

Subscribing means getting out your credit card and paying, usually for one or more months of membership on the site. If you buy a block of three or six months the monthly price goes down. Most sites automatically renew (and bill) you at the end of that time period, unless you go to your account page and set it to non-renewal, which is easy to do. (A notable exception here is Lavalife.com, which has a pay-as-you-go structure; you buy credits as you want/need to use them, and there is no automatic renewal.)[1]

Let's look more closely at these three steps. (In order to keep things simple I won't delve yet into the fine points of one site's features versus another's—that will come a little later when I survey four major sites.)

SCANNING

Even before you sign up, you can navigate around a site and check out the lay of the land. Most major sites will also let you

---

1. At the time of this writing, Yahoo! Personals is $24.95 per month, Match.com $29.99. If you subscribe for three months they go down to around $17 per month, for six months $12.50 and $15 respectively. You can get started on Lavalife for a mere $14.99 for 50 credits. The heavy-duty matchmaking sites (such as eHarmony.com) cost more: eHarmony starts at $59.95 if you only commit to one month; Chemistry.com at $49.95. All pricing figures are of course subject to change by the vendor.

start searching. In fact, they will usher you into a basic search right away, because the existence of desirable members is the lure they want you to see.

SIGNING UP

You've looked around, and now you are interested enough in a site to take a little time and effort.

You create a username (it must be unique) and a password. Then, as part of signing up you provide an e-mail address, so that the dating site can communicate with you, and as an assurance of sincerity. This e-mail address will generally not be visible to site members when you exchange e-mails with them within the site. If, even knowing that, you don't want the site to have your main/home e-mail address (which may contain your name), it is easy to create free e-mail "identities" on such portals as Yahoo!, MSN Hotmail, and the newly free AOL, that you access online and that are not linked in any way to your "home" e-mail.

Now it's time to create your profile. First you answer a bunch of multiple-choice questions about yourself on topics like age, gender, appearance, lifestyle, income, and interests. The major sites have lots of parameters for you to fill in, which won't seem like a chore when you realize that you're helping Mr. Right find you, and his answers to the same questions will help you find him.

Next come the little "personal pieces" that I mentioned earlier. In the main one, you describe yourself and the person you seek: it has different labels on different sites but I will call it your Introduction. In the other short pieces you delight the reader with your thoughts on other facets of your life. To top it all off, you also create a catchy headline. With the possible exception of your photos, these "In Your Own Words" pieces are the most important part of your ad, because they contain the unique flavour of you, and they allow you to speak directly to the person you are trying to meet. I will give detailed tips on how to construct a good Introduction. Bear in mind if you are trying several sites, that once you have a good Introduction written, you can copy it from one site to another—you don't have to reinvent the wheel.

Your self-written pieces are the most important part of your ad, because they contain the unique flavour of you, and they allow you to speak directly to the person you are trying to meet.

The final piece of the puzzle is your photo. Dating sites don't insist that you provide one, but there are very powerful reasons why you should—unless you don't really want to find a good partner! In fact you should post at least two photos, a head-shot and a full-length shot. And it isn't enough just to grab any old pics. They are going to be Mr. Right's first look at you—and perhaps his only look if they don't do you justice. I devote two chapters to this visual opportunity, and how and why you should embrace it.

SUBSCRIBING

You can sign up and create your profile without yet subscribing. Dating sites encourage you to do this, because they think it moves you one step closer to being a paying customer, and they think that the more you learn about their features, the more likely you are to commit your dollars. Now obviously they have to hold something back: They can't let you do *everything* without paying! The surprise is how far they will let you go before you haul out the plastic. Let's look at that.

LOOK BEFORE YOU PAY

The Joys of Free Searching

"*You* pays your money and you takes your chances," some-one once said.

The nice thing about online dating is that it isn't like that. Egged on by their own foolish optimism, many dating sites allow you to take a serious look at their facilities *and their members*, before you pay any fee.

And that is my advice. Test several sites before you sub-scribe to any. In particular, try a few searches. See if you like the search features and the way members are presented. Above all, look closely at the men who come up in your search re-sults. Are any of them the sort of guy you're looking for? If so, do the same test on some other sites. There's no reason why you should cough up any bucks before you develop a level of confidence.

Let's get an overview of the searching process, and see what searches you can do for free on major sites, and what costs money.

Chapter 21

SEARCH PARAMETERS AND SEARCH RESULTS

If a keyword search on calamari doesn't locate the seafood-loving guy you're seeking, try lobster.

When you do a basic search (sometimes called browsing), you specify several characteristics of the person you are looking for—age range, gender, and nearness to your location. After an amazingly short pause, the site presents you with a display of members who meet those requirements. In addition to those three parameters, the basic search usually involves two interesting boxes to check or not check. Box one restricts the search to people *who are actually online right now*. Box two restricts the search to people *who have posted photos*. After you have looked at a few ads with photos, you are likely to check the latter box, because *you will realize that you find the photos very relevant*. Mr. Right is even more likely to check the photo box, as we'll see when we look deeper into the photo issue. For now, notice that if you don't post a photo, and if Mr. Right checks that little box, he will never find you. All three of the top sites we are going to depict allow you to do a basic search without even signing up (let alone subscribing).

ADVANCED SEARCH

So much for the basic search. You are very likely going to want to specify some more points about your wished-for partner. For example, you may wish to look for a man who has at least a certain education level, a certain income, perhaps certain interests, a certain attitude to having children, maybe some political or religious stance, maybe some physical features. When you add such particulars, you are creating an advanced or customized search. On Yahoo! Personals it is possible to bring as many as thirty-four parameters to bear.

But wait, that's not all! Many sites will allow you to do special "matching" searches, or will do these for you and even e-mail you the results as often as you want. These searches look for people who have what you want, *and* want what you have. That's a *mutual* search. Match.com also offers a "reverse" search, where they look for members who are looking for your characteristics, but who don't necessarily meet your specifications. An intriguing detour into realism...

You can usually save advanced searches by giving them a name of your choosing, so you can easily repeat them in future.

KEYWORD SEARCH

And that's still not all. If you're willing to go on a bit of a fishing expedition, there is another clever trick that can be fun to try. It's called a *keyword search*. Keyword searching looks at the words that members wrote themselves in their Introduction and other sections. You specify a word or words you are interested in, and the search finds people who used that word. This is a powerful feature because it allows you to delve into the most personal and original portions of users' profiles, and find the gold you seek. A keyword search can get fairly whimsical: search on Scorsese, search on chopper, search on calamari. If calamari doesn't locate the seafood-loving guy you're seeking, try lobster.[1]

Match.com and Yahoo! Personals will both allow you to do their most elaborate searches *without even signing up*. Lavalife is more "demanding": They'll give you the basic search, but if you want the custom search you have to sign up. None of

---

1. Some sites won't give you their advanced search capabilities until you pay: This is true, for example, of the Friendfinder.com family of sites, which is nevertheless worth looking at and does allow you to browse without subscribing.

these sites demands that you subscribe (pay anything) to test out their full searches, though Match.com won't show you a person's whole profile until you create one yourself.

A Searching Tip

A word of caution regarding search strategy. As you probably know, the more you specify in a search, the fewer hits you are going to get. So don't go overboard. Start with facets of a person that are very important to you, the lack of which would be a deal-breaker. Otherwise you may overlook someone who has the important things you want but lacks some unimportant thing! If you find you're getting too many hits, you can try adding more characteristics later.

Conversely, if you're going to specify a given area, be as inclusive as you can. Bear in mind that some of these multiple-choice questions are not that easy to answer. Mr. Right may not have given the response you think, so you could inadvertently exclude him from your search!

He agonizes for five seconds because "Slim" sounds to him like a ranch hand in an old Western, "slender" sounds like a girl, and "average" sounds... average.

For example, when Mr. Jones did his profile, he had to choose a body type for himself. Two of the choices on Yahoo! Personals are "fit" and "athletic." There are also "slim" and "slender," and a bunch of others. Now Jones is a lean fellow who takes brisk walks three times a week and plays tennis occasionally with a pretty decent backhand. What should he say? Is he slim or slender? Is he fit or athletic? He can only choose one of the four! Suppose he agonizes for five seconds because "slim" sounds to him like a ranch hand in an old Western, "slender" sounds like a girl, and "average" sounds... average. There's no way to say lean that he likes. So he goes for "fit".

Then Ms. Smith comes along doing a search, and she is in the mood for a thin or average guy, so in her search she checks average and slim (she too doesn't like the sound of slender for a guy). She doesn't check fit or athletic, because she's afraid this may represent rabid sports and fitness buffs, of which she isn't one. So Mr. Jones doesn't come up on her search; and she never sees his fabulous profile which, after saying a whole lot that would have rung loud bells for her, adds the line, "By the way, I'm not obsessed with exercise, I just like walking." The moral: Take advantage of categories that allow you to check more than one choice. Check *all the options that could conceivably apply*, or check "any" so none are excluded. And be careful of categories that force you to choose only one answer—sometimes it's better to leave them out of your search.

SEARCH RESULTS

The results of your search will appear in two main ways. One is the profile summary with a photo beside it: That's usually the default. The other is a photo gallery that displays a lot more people per screen by showing *only their photos*. From a photo you can go to further photos of that person or to their full profile. Many sites also allow you to block a given member from showing up on future searches, so you don't keep seeing people you've decided you're not interested in.

Many sites allow you to add members you like to a "Favourites" list, and to view those who have added you to theirs. This allows you to find people who have taken a shine to you but haven't tried to contact you—sort of a form of playing hard to get... Another feature found on most good sites is the ability to sort or search by how recently the person has been active on the site, allowing you to avoid defunct members who are no longer looking.

CONTACT WITH OTHER MEMBERS: THE MONEY LINE

Finally, the search results screen offers you various ways to contact someone. You can send them a wink, which lets them know you're interested and to which they may reply. You can send them an e-mail. And on some sites you can Instant Message them.

And here at last we arrive at the money line. On most sites you can send a wink without being a subscriber. But if you want to be able to send e-mails or IMs and reply to same, you need to subscribe and pay the fee. This is only fair, since otherwise you could drag Mr. Right home and never have paid a cent!

The exact rules as to when you cross the money line differ from one site to another, but the main point is clear: When you want full privileges of contacting and replying to other members of the site, you need to be a subscriber.

Warning: Watch out for "free trials" on dating sites. They may be for as little as seven days or just a weekend, and in order to use them you have to provide your credit card info. *That means that if you don't cancel, you'll be charged for an automatic renewal after the free period is over.* If you go for a free trial, make sure you keep track of the days, know exactly how to access the cancellation menu, and do so in time.

Before we tour some notable dating sites, let's go back to the two main pieces of your online presentation: the profile and the photos. I'll offer some tips on making both of them maximally effective.

HEADLINE AND INTRODUCTION

How to Make Them Sing

*I*t's time to get down to brass tacks, as my grandma used to say. Your Introduction is a portrait of you and the man you seek, in your own words. Your headline is the hook. What are the dos and don'ts of writing them?

Don't underestimate the challenge of this kind of writing. What you're creating is an online ad. If advertising were easy, giant corporations would not be paying millions of dollars to those who create fifteen-second TV spots. Advertising is in fact an art form, one that uses the finest human gifts, often in service of not-so-fine motives.

The good news is that your online ad is in service of love. If you follow a few simple guidelines, you can use your own talent to project a zesty image of yourself, that will attract just the suitors you want.

Let's assume that Mr. Right-for-you is sitting in front of his computer and has just done a search on a dating site. Maybe he's browsing—looking at women in a certain age range in his area—or maybe he's done an advanced search to narrow it down more. Now he looks through the search results, trying to find you. As we discussed earlier, he either looks at a pho-to gallery, or at photos accompanied by the headline and the opening lines of the Introduction.

What many a man does is this: He looks through the pho-tos until he sees one that interests him; then he looks at the headline and Introduction to get a sense of who this person is. This is the moment when the headline means the most. If he is still interested, he will open up the profile and look at ev-erything: your multiple-choice info, your other photos if any, and your self-penned Introduction and other short bits. When Mr. Right reaches this stage, the single thing that is going to matter most to him is your Introduction, because that is his first chance to hear your unique "voice." As one man whom I interviewed put it: "A photo can attract you, but the Intro has the soul."

We'll look at the headline first.

BEFORE THE AD, COMES THE HEADLINE
Let's look at how to create a good one.

The best way to start is to browse through a bunch of head-lines written by others. It may be more fun for you to peruse men's headlines; but it may be more instructive to look at those of other women.

Let's survey some sample headlines, and ask ourselves what is right or wrong with them.

For the sake of entertainment (especially for those who like puzzles), I will present headlines in groups, then I'll diag-nose their problems.[1]

---

1. All headlines I discuss are made up by me to illustrate a point.

Check out these banners:

- Looking for Someone Like You
- Something Different
- Seeking Mr. Right
- Someone Special
- Are You My Type?
- Fun Gal Seeks Fun Guy
- Are You Looking for Me?

If you want to convey how much fun you are, make up a headline that is fun to read.

Does the word "vague" come to mind? It is great to offer "something different," but that phrase alone tells us nothing about what is being offered, or how it's different. All of these headlines *lack specifics*, and specifics are the fuel that makes good writing run. It is as if you picked up this morning's newspaper and the front page announced, "Something Happened Somewhere." It may be true but it ain't too grabby. You might think the author of this book would approve of the headline "Seeking Mr. Right"—but I don't. The problem is, it doesn't tell us how this person defines Mr. Right.

Looking at it another way, there is no point in saying you are looking for Mr. Right, because it prompts the response, "Isn't everybody? Tell me something I don't know."

Consider these offerings:

- Looking for a Kindred Spirit
- Not Average or Typical
- Seeking Chemistry
- Attractive, Fun-loving Woman
- This is Me

The problem here is that all these headlines state obvious truths—what they say goes without saying. Aren't we *all* looking for a kindred spirit? Don't we all think we are not average or typical? It is important not to present yourself in a typical way, or an average way; but merely stating that one is not average doesn't cut it. Most people think they are attractive, and most people claim to love fun. If you want to convey how much fun you are, make up a headline that is fun to read.

As the great American novelist Henry James advised his fellow writers: "Don't just tell us; *show* us!"

So far we have discussed problems of style. Here are some headlines that commit a slightly different and more dangerous sin, one that gets into psychology:

- RU Attractive?
- Looking for a Great Sense of Humour!
- Just Looking for a Nice Guy
- Seeking One Good Man

Remember give-away questions on exams in school? Questions that practically begged for a certain answer. These headlines are like that. All men are going to answer them the same way. What self-respecting male *isn't* going to say he's attractive, nice, good, and has a great sense of humour? Even if he's dishonest, repulsive, and never laughs, he is not going to miss a pitch that is lobbed right over the middle of the plate, like these. Again, if you want to find someone with a good sense of humour—or even better, a sense of humour akin to your own—then the best thing to do is to compose an ad that is funny, in your own unique way. Then the right men will laugh at it and be curious to know more about you.

Consider these nuggets:

- Not into Games
- Liars Need Not Apply
- Honest Woman; Honest Man?
- Sick of Cheaters

They don't mean to, but these headlines carry a big "victim" sign. The shrewd male who reads them can easily figure out that this woman is coming out of a bad relationship where she got victimized by a guy who lied and cheated; and now she is seeking the antidote to that poison. The trouble is, she sounds paranoid, like she's going to scrutinize every man she meets for the telltale signs of dishonesty. She is obsessed with trust. Therefore she is perfect prey for the dishonest man. (See my discussion of trust in Chapter 10.)

Here is another miscue:

- This is My First Time
- I Can't Believe I'm Doing This!
- Don't Tell My Mom

It's obvious, isn't it? Don't express embarrassment that you are advertising on a dating site. Better to lead from strength, and get to something interesting.

Two more gems:

- Is Mr. Right Even Out There?
- Don't Judge this Book by its Cover

Both of these lines reveal pessimism and hint at a loser's history.

I think you get the point. We need your headline to be positive, specific, optimistic, and confident. That doesn't mean it has to be brilliant or super-clever. If you can manage to be unique and original, so much the better. Just go with your strong suit. And have fun writing it.

Let's look at some good headlines, to inspire you. After each one I'll say what works about it:

- Love Being Outdoors (This is simple but positive, sincere and specific.)
- Chemist Seeks Lab Assistant (Intriguing: Is she really a chemist, or is it a metaphor?)
- Svelte Blonde into Sitcoms (This sounds honest.)
- SWF for SBM (It's not original, but at least it's specific.)
- Notorious Seeks Vertigo (This will appeal to a movie lover.)
- Tree-hugging Liberal Seeks Same (Self-deprecating honesty never is bad.)
- Glamorous Executive Seeks Handyman (This paints a picture.)
- Seeking Dom/Sub Adventures with Biker (If you walk on the wild side, say so.)
- Listener Seeks Talker (This is quirky and charming.)
- Zaftig and Brainy (If you've got a lethal combo, mention it.)
- Witty Actress (Covers a lot in two words.)

One more suggestion: Start by asking yourself how well your photo presents you. If you are very confident that it does the job, then maybe you should consider using your headline to describe the guy you're looking for. If you're not so sure your photo conveys your uniqueness, then let your headline capture *you*. You can always go into detail about the man you seek in your Introduction. Which leads us to that topic.

TEN EASY STEPS TO A GREAT INTRODUCTION

Your Introduction is easier to write than your headline because you don't have to compress everything down to a few words. You can take off your advertising hat and put on your letter-writing hat, because an Introduction is really a letter from you to the man you seek. It's your chance to talk openly and naturally, the way you really talk, to the man you are looking for.

What self-respecting male isn't going to say he's attractive, nice, good, and has a great sense of humour?

Some of our headline tips apply here too. Don't start by saying how awkward or difficult it is to write about yourself. Skip ahead to the good stuff. Don't hang a "victim" sign on yourself by saying you're tired of games and want an honest man. You can attract more honest people by *being* honest than by *saying* you want honesty.

And now to our tips:

Be yourself. You don't have to appeal to the world at large, it doesn't matter whether seven out of ten men like what you have to say. What matters is that you sound like you, so a guy who is looking for you will recognize the woman he seeks.

Picture your reader. Think whom you are writing to. Have you ever noticed that when you write a letter, your thoughts come out differently depending on who you're writing to? But when you try to write to no one or everyone, it gets stilted?

So remember that you are writing to Mr. Right, *your* Mr. Right, not anyone else's. A man who will relish you in all your uniqueness, a man whom you will savour. He already likes you; he just hasn't met you yet. Trust him. Talk to *him*. You may be surprised at how easily the words flow.

Talk about the things in your life that move you. They can be positive but they can be negative too. Things that thrill you, things that irritate the hell out of you. (Lots of people enjoy someone who is annoyed by the same things they are.) Stay away from neutral topics.

Be honest. Describe yourself, physically, mentally, your lifestyle, where you are on the journey. Don't try to sell yourself—you don't have to because you are pre-sold to this man.

Don't hang a "victim" sign on yourself by saying you're tired of games and want an honest man.

Which raises an interesting point. Should you reveal things in your Intro that are likely to make some men turn away? The answer is yes, if they are things that matter to you. The man you want will become *more* interested. The beauty of honest profiles is that long before you actually meet, you've both had a chance to lay your big cards on the table. Thus you avoid the pain of dealing in person with someone who doesn't like those cards. If you have two boys and want a man who is open to becoming their parent, say so. The man you are looking for will see this as a plus.

Distinguish yourself. Ask yourself, what makes me different from everybody else? Then talk about that.

Don't try to be clever. Be clever. Use your natural sense of play when it fits. There is nothing like wit and humour to give the reader a flavour of you.

Share your hopes. You probably already know what things you hope to share with your partner. Go into them. If you want to tour the west in a Winnebago, say so. If you like doing team commentary on the soap opera that is your friends' lives, say so, and give juicy examples.

Latch on to the negative. If you know what sort of man or relationship you aren't looking for, talk about that. Especially if it's commonly sought. Use your profile to weed people out, and you will save yourself a lot of wasted effort. If you don't want a man who likes sitcoms, say so. If there are specific types of response that you've been getting but you don't want, mention them in a clear, non-hostile way. This approach is really helpful because it'll discourage the responses you don't want, and it'll excite the people who are like you, who share your values. A lot of people like the same things: What you don't like will pinpoint your uniqueness.

Be creative. A helpful exercise: Use your imagination and write the profile you wish your man would write, that you would find in his ad. Then think about what you can put in your profile that such a man would want to read.

Be specific. Don't talk about flowers, mention wild asters. Don't say you love comedy, mention Mad TV or *Wedding Crashers.*

23

PHOTO PHILOSOPHY

Why You Need to Post Photos

In the next chapter I talk about how to do a good photo set. But first let's look at the good reasons why you should include photos with your profile, and the shaky reasons that are sometimes given for not doing this.

The top reason for posting a photo: People online are *much* more likely to look at an ad if it has a photo. According to Match.com, men are fifteen times more likely to look at ads with photos; women are eight times more likely. Most people start with the photos: That is their entrée into the profiles. When browsing or searching, it is very easy to check the box that says "photos only." So most people don't even look at ads that lack photos.

If you try the other approach, you'll find it has its pitfalls. Suppose you find a guy whose profile seems engaging. He didn't post a photo, but what the hey, he says he's a dead ringer for Brad Pitt. So you start e-mailing and talking on the phone, and pretty soon you're letting yourself get involved, though you haven't even met. Then one drizzly morning he sends you a photo, taken with his brand new digital camera. And you get a rude awakening: He looks like Brad Pitt's dissolute cousin. The photo immediately explodes your fantasy, and now you have to backtrack like mad.

It only takes a few experiences like this to make you very wary of books with no illustrations. You realize it's always better to get issues of basic physical appearance out of the way as early as possible. And somewhere out there on the web, Mr. Right-for-you realizes it too.

"Beauty is in the eye of the beholder," we have always been told. On the Internet this translates into a piece of hard-hitting street-wisdom:

Don't let someone else tell you whether you will find them attractive, because they don't know.

Then one drizzly morning he sends you a photo, and he looks like Brad Pitt's dissolute cousin.

The decision has to be yours. (Conversely, don't expect a man to believe you if you say you're a head-turner but refuse to send him a photo.) The happy truth is that most people who enjoy passable mental health think themselves attractive, and in fact they *are* attractive to someone; but that doesn't mean they will be attractive to *you*.

Of course, I admit that you can't always tell from a photo that you will find someone attractive; but believe me, you can often tell that you won't!

Enter the résistance. In my research I ran across some interesting reasons for not wanting to post a photo on a dating site.

- Love should be based on inner qualities, and so should the sexual aspect of love. So Mr. Right shouldn't need to see me.

- I don't have any good photos of myself; I'm always the one *behind* the camera.
- It's too much trouble to get a good photo taken. I wouldn't know where to begin.
- I'm not photogenic.

Let me offer some thoughts in response.

Every day as you walk through this world, you share your visual self with anyone who happens to be in the vicinity. Every time you meet a new person, you let them look upon you. You let them see your clothed body and your face. So if you are exploring a potential mate online, you should extend each other the same courtesy, with the help of photographs. After all, you are going to meet in person eventually. That is the goal here. At that point all will be visible. So make sure there won't be any big surprises.

As to the next two reasons: Those who are not willing to invest the time and effort it takes to obtain a couple of good pictures of themselves are not serious about finding a mate.

The happy truth is that most people who enjoy passable mental health think themselves attractive.

The objection "I'm not photogenic" may mask a worse fear, leading to a deeper pitfall. Some people may think, "I can't compete with the gorgeous folks; I'm plain. So I will win a person over with my fabulous mind and my generous heart, as communicated in my brilliant e-mails and IMs; then when I finally spring my appearance on them it will be too late for them to escape, they will be hooked." Thus the Internet becomes a tool of deception, a way of *securing the attention of people one thinks one could not attract in person.* But this is not honest, not effective, and not necessary. Because eventually the goal is to stand face to face; or if it isn't, one is playing a bizarre game.

Anyway, as we saw earlier, there is more to "looks" than being "good-looking." We all rely on visual perception to tell us a whole lot about the people we encounter. Men see a whole person in a woman's face, including qualities of character, heart, and mind. Even on a sexual level, different men are attracted to different faces and body types: There is no universal standard.

If you don't think you are a raving beauty, take further comfort in the fact that there are many men who could never really feel secure with an extremely good-looking woman, because either they've been burned by women like that in the past, they are threatened by the interest she arouses in other men, or they don't think of themselves as great lookers.

The bottom line: A man who is right for you *will* find you appealing, but only if you let him see you.

Finally, what about sexual attraction? Is it really a rational thing based solely on what's inside? Should photos be irrelevant to it? Here are some thoughts:

- Sexual attraction has an irrational component. It is not based solely on how much you like someone as a person. It isn't based on personal merit, or niceness, or giving to the right charities, or liking the right rock bands. The proof is obvious: We have all had close friends (of the other gender) with whom we had no chemistry. In fact, if sexuality were rational, we would all be sleeping with our best friends, regardless of gender.

- Sexual attraction is, in fact, so independent of our best values, that it frequently causes people to make disastrous choices, that wreck their lives and those of others—this is true right up to the Oval Office. A million sad love songs are not wrong.

- Sexual attraction cannot be established just from information conveyed in words. You may learn through e-mails or IMs that someone shares your sexual interests or even style. But any torch you have lit may fizzle the first time you see that person. Of course you'll also need to hear his voice; to hold, smell, feel, kiss, and make love with him. At some point, sexual attraction must defer to something greater (sexual compatibility); but attraction is still necessary.

- If you find it unpleasant to gaze upon someone—if that person's shape, size, style, or features simply turn you off —he is unlikely to be the right mate for you.

Sexual attraction is so independent of our best values, that it frequently causes people to make disastrous choices, that wreck their lives and those of others—this is true right up to the Oval Office.

I am not claiming that you can always ascertain physical attractiveness from a photo. What I am saying is, *you can often detect its absence.* You can often tell from a good photo that this particular person is not attractive to you. And that information is priceless! It can save you months of futile pursuit.

So there we have it. People need to see each other, by way of good photographs, as early as possible. The woman who realizes this and facilitates it, has taken a major step towards the man she seeks. So it behooves us to look more closely at this tool.

24

A GOOD PHOTO

What to Shoot For

$\mathcal{H}$ere are the basics, without which a photo does not pass muster.

A GOOD PHOTO MUST BE RECENT

It is amazing how many people online try to get away with sending obsolete pictures of themselves. "This is the way I wish I still looked," they might as well say.

Harry sends Sally a photo showing a smooth-skinned, handsome brute with wavy brown hair and a lean build. He gives his height as 5' 10". After two months of talking online and on the phone, Sally meets Harry. She walks into a local café and can't figure out which man could be him: The attractive guy in the corner has blond hair, so he can't be the one. Then the pudgy, aging bald man near the door stands up and smiles at Sally. He is about 5' 2". And her heart sinks: Not because she couldn't like a man who looked like this, but because she has been lied to. Harry sent a fifteen-year-old picture (and lied about his height).

Don't use the excuse, "I have no recent shots of myself." Take the trouble to get a good photo. If you have a good one that is a year or two old, that may be OK, if you still look like it. If not, get a new one.

A GOOD PHOTO MUST BE ACCURATE, NOT MISLEADING, AND MUST LOOK LIKE YOU

Every now and then, everyone has a picture taken that looks fabulous, but, unfortunately, doesn't look like her. The lighting, or the moment, or the angle, was such that Helen Smith could be mistaken for Greta Garbo. Unfortunately, in real life Helen never is mistaken for Greta Garbo. So Helen shouldn't use that photo online.

The goal *is to give the recipient an experience as close as possible to what they would see if they actually met you, in normal circumstances.*

A GOOD PHOTO MUST BE FAVOURABLE

People like Jude Law and Halle Berry don't have to worry, they always look great. Bone structure like that cannot be missed. That is why they are movie stars. But most of us look good some of the time, and it never seems to be when a camera is pointed at us. (Have you noticed: You often seem to look good in the bathroom mirror? That is because you [and I] have practiced every day for years, posing in front of it.)

So you should choose a photo that captures you looking good. Not flattering. Favourable.

Remember, you are used to seeing yourself backwards (in the mirror). Therefore a good portrait of you may seem to you to have a disturbingly lopsided face—because you have learned to accept the asymmetry the other way. Don't be alarmed. If necessary, hold the photo up to a mirror, and be reassured that it captures the good-looking "you" that you are familiar with.

If you don't already have one, a favourable photo can be hard to come by. You need someone to take it.

THE IDEAL PHOTOGRAPHER IS

- Someone you trust, so you will relax. Most of us look best when we are comfortable, able to smile naturally.
- Someone with an eye. Some people, while looking through a camera's viewfinder, are able to see what the photo will look like. And to see when you are looking best and press the button. These people are invaluable.
- Someone who will direct you. "Tilt your chin up a bit. Now turn your head.... Yeah, that's good. Now, think of napoleon pastries..."
- A professional? Well, maybe. You don't want something really slick and stilted and artificial looking. Most professional photo studios turn out an absurd product. They make everyone look the same: shiny, ethereal, phony. Like they died and went to Photo Heaven. Such a photo may be very impressive to some tastes, but it doesn't look natural, or real. On the other hand, if you know someone who takes photographs as an *artist*, rush to them and ask for this favour.
- Someone who will take a lot of shots. On a day when you feel OK with your bad self, let someone you know—a friend, an ex-lover, your child—whoever it is, let them take a lot of pictures. Keep on shooting, while you are going about your business. If it's a digital camera, you can always delete the unused ones; if it isn't, invest in a couple of rolls. Shoot

some that are carefully posed, some when you don't even notice it's being taken. Be yourself. The more photos you have taken, the more likely it is that one or two of them will leap to your eye and make you say, "Yes, that's me."

A GOOD PHOTO MUST BE A GLAMOUR SHOT? NOT SO MUCH.

Don't rush to the nearest shopping mall and line up for a glamour shot. Such photos, with their sex-kitten furs and loud makeup, are a form of disguise. They aren't going to prepare anyone for the experience of seeing you in real life. (Unless of course, that *is* the normal you! In which case, don't hold back.)

A GOOD PHOTO MUST SHOW YOU IN THE SUN? WRONG.

The worst place to take a portrait of you is standing outside in the bright sun. The poor guy who looks at it can only tell that you are someone squinting. He can't see what you look like. He can't see your beautiful eyes. I have even seen pictures in which people wear shades. Don't.

A PHOTO MUST BE WELL LIT, IN FOCUS.

So take the photo outdoors in shade, or indoors in nice light, or anywhere that lets the camera capture your face. Often indoor shots near a window are good, with natural light pouring in—but let it be diffuse, not direct sunlight.

A GOOD PHOTO IS PART OF A GOOD PHOTO SET—ONE HEAD-SHOT AND ONE FULL-LENGTH SHOT, AT LEAST.

You need both. The head-shot gives the portrait of your soulful face. The full-length shot shows off your colour sense and style. It also tells the truth about your size and shape, so those matters can be gotten out of the way up front. Let two honest photos do the work for you: If he is still interested after he sees them, then you have something real to build on.

If he isn't, you are so much better off knowing now.

On today's dating sites, many women and men supply photo sets with three, four, or more photos. Two has become the minimum. Note: If you don't wish to share your additional photos with just any visitor to the site, Lavalife has a "Backstage" feature, where only your main photo is visible to members unless you specifically grant them access. I discuss this when I tour top sites, shortly.

What should you wear in the full-length photo? A good rule of thumb is: whatever you would wear if you were meeting him for the first time in a café.

*W*anda and Fred had talked on line for three months, by e-mail and IM. He had asked to meet her but she was hesitant, and busy... and maybe she was trying to avoid facing what she already guessed would happen. The thing was, Wanda really liked Fred. He was so many things that aroused her dreams: He was articulate, well-off, gentlemanly, and funny. Sometimes they talked on the phone and she loved his deep, cuddly voice. He had willingly sent her a picture and she thought him very handsome—he reminded her of a darker, younger Robert Redford. So she began early to weave a web, one that caught him, and more importantly, caught herself. They got more and more romantic, she was in Swoonville. She told him she had no photo: She said, "It's crazy, but I'm always the one *taking* the picture..." When he asked what she looked like, she stressed the positive things, her pretty face and her long legs. What was not to like?

The only trouble was, she never implied in any way that she weighed any more than 140. Even though Fred had casually mentioned that he was very fit, and liked athletic women. After all, Wanda reasoned, I'm athletic, I've got a pretty mean crawl in the old swimming pool.

So they met, finally, at an expensive restaurant with white tablecloths and candles—because nothing less seemed right for two people so in love.

They met, and Fred turned into the anti-Fred. He was cold, distant, not funny, and impatient; when the meal finally came it seemed to last three months. Conversation didn't flow. He never tried to take her hand; they parted awkwardly.

She began early to weave a web, one that caught him, and more importantly, caught herself.

Days later Wanda ran into him online and had the courage to ask him what had gone wrong. For a moment his words suggested the old Fred, then he finally said, "I'm sorry but I am just not attracted to larger women." Wanda made an angry reply, something to the effect of "Thanks for pretending that you care about what's inside a person," and got offline. Later she cried with anger. It took her a long time to see that the anger was mostly directed at herself.

Wanda was a beautiful woman who weighed 190 and carried that weight very well. There are plenty of men out there who want a woman like Wanda.

But Fred wasn't one of them.

She had wasted her own time and emotion, and his too.

Summing up:

Be honest and informative about your looks, weight, and body type and expect the same from men you meet online.

In these ways you will make sure that the men you spend time on are men whose definition of "attractive" you fit, and vice versa.

So you can move on to other, more profound issues, serene in the knowledge that your efforts won't all be wasted by a matter of appearances.

USE THE INTERNET TO SET YOURSELF FREE

A final thought. As we have seen earlier, our media culture tries to humiliate women who are normal-sized or larger. (The same forces are now expanding their war to undermine men too.) I tried in Part Two to poke holes in this propaganda, and fortunately I have as allies the makers of Dove Soap and many wiser writers on this topic, who have provided pathways that can help all of us resist the indoctrination and love our bodies.

What I want to add is this: Don't use the Internet to aid and abet negative attitudes to your physical self. Use it to set yourself free. Consider these facts:

- The Internet has made it obvious that the fuller female form has plenty of male admirers—it has brought these men out of the closet, and allowed them to admit that they desire women who are different from the stereotypes of fashion ads and sitcom leads. According to some surveys, over forty percent of men like larger women.[1]
- The Internet has made it possible for women to band together with their sisters who want to celebrate the joys of being bountiful...there are endless chat rooms, Web sites,

---

1. The term BBW (Big Beautiful Woman) has had a colourful history on the Internet, being originally coined to encourage larger women to feel good about themselves. Many sites (some very respectable, some naughty) are devoted to BBWs and their admirers. Two of the best dating sites are BBWdatefinder.com and BBWPersonalsPlus.com.

Web rings, and bulletin boards devoted to these topics.

- The Internet has made it easy for men and women of whatever physical type to find, and be found by, those who like that type.
- There is no better antidote to doubts about your body than living with someone who genuinely admires it.

So be brave enough to stand on the truth; present yourself as you are, and expect the same from men. Then sit back and let nature take its course. Use the Internet as a vehicle to carry you to the House of Acceptance: where two people live together, loving each other, and knowing that the other person is not trying to change them into something else.

26

CHOOSING A DATING SITE

A Portrait of Three Top Sites

$\mathcal{I}$'ve talked about how to do a little prospecting on major dating sites before you subscribe. It's also a good idea to take a look at a few sites of other kinds.

Niche sites exist for almost any persuasion. The Friendfinder-.com line, in addition to its main site, contains separate sites for seniors, gays, Christians, Jewish people, adult encounters, and more. Elsewhere on the Web there are sites like SingleParentMeet-.com, BlackPeopleMeet.com, BBWDatefinder.com, JDate.com (Jewish singles), Gay.com, DateMyPet.com, CyclingSingles.com, TatooedSingles.com, sites for admirers of Ayn Rand's novels (TheAtlasphere.com), scuba divers (ScubaDivingSingles.com), and geeks (gk2gk.com). If you do a Google search on "dating site for x" and fill in x with the category of your choice, you will probably find something.

Then there are free dating sites. The leader here is the aptly named PlentyOfFish.com, started in 2003 in Canada and already in the top five of free *and paid* Canadian sites, and fast rising elsewhere. The look of PlentyOfFish is not as lavish as that of the paid sites, it isn't as detailed in its parameters, and it lacks many bells and whistles. For example, you can't restrict search results to those with photos (which some may see as a plus); profiles and matching have fewer parameters; and keyword searching is limited to the "interests" field. But PlentyOfFish gets the basic job done, and it's free. If free is really a virtue. Some argue that paid sites attract more serious people: The cost acts as a screening device.

Another type of free site is the *social networking* site à la MySpace.com. MySpace was founded in July 2003 and rapidly grew into the monster it is today, having surpassed one hundred million accounts. It features blogs, member profiles, photos, and videos, also functioning as a showcase and proving ground for indie music and film. There is a lot of emphasis on building a network of friends who are proudly displayed on one's own MySpace site. It is not a dedicated dating site, but there is no doubt that it acts as one, among its many roles. It tends to skew towards teens and young adults. See also Youtube.com.

And now it's time to take a tour of some of the top non-free dating sites. Rather than trot out a confusing chart with an endless list of features, I'm going to present a quick portrait of each site, pointing out things I think are worthy of note.

MATCH.COM: LAVISH AND WELL THOUGHT-OUT
One of the oldest and biggest dating sites on the planet, Match.com was launched in 1995 and now has over fifteen million members and over a million subscribers. It has local sites in more than thirty countries and is among the top sites in Canada and the US (match.com), in the UK (uk.match.com) and in Australia (au.match.com).

When you fill out your profile on Match.com you will find yourself giving multiple-choice answers in up to fifty areas—thirty-three concerning you and seventeen the person you are seeking—in such areas as appearance, interests, lifestyle, and background/values. You can also rate each aspect of your intended mate as to how important it is to you. In addition you compose your Introduction and you can write little pieces on topics such as what you do for fun, travel spots that appeal to you, favourite things, and what you last read.

It can be both humbling and encouraging to take a break from your own wish list and see whose wish list you are on.

The result is a lavishly detailed portrait of each member and their intended mate that allows searching to be very powerful. There are several noteworthy types of search. The advanced search lets you wallow in parameters. When you have a search you want to repeat in future, you can name and save it. You can limit searches to people online now, or to people with photos. There is a keyword search, which looks in the text that members wrote themselves for whatever words you specify. It is an interesting way of fishing, and it often has great results. If you are obsessed with Dostoevsky, you can find someone else who is.

In addition Match.com has created a feature called "MatchWords," where you can tailor your own list of "catch" words, whether or not you used them in your Introduction. Examples would be ethnic, kayak, poetry, linguini. When you spot a MatchWord you like in search results, you can press it to get to other profiles that contain it.

Two other searches are offered that find members who match, based on their profiles. The mutual search finds people whose profiles agree with what you are looking for, and *vice versa*; the reverse search shows you members who are looking for a profile like yours. It can be both humbling and encouraging to take a break from your own wish list and see whose wish list you are on.

A notable virtue of Match.com is its handling of the *body type* parameter. Many sites offer a few choices intended to cover both men and women, with very blunt results. They obsess on weight as if it were the only factor in body type, ignoring shape. They use negative words. It can be very hard for the user to locate themselves on this menu, and often they are forced to either be dishonest or put themselves down. A choice between "average," "slightly overweight," and "large" can be a hard one to make. Match.com rides to the rescue here by offering different words to men and women, and letting those words be more positive. Bigger men are offered "stocky" and "heavyset" in addition to "a few extra pounds"; women are offered "curvy," "full figured," and "big and beautiful."

A choice between "average," "slightly overweight," and "large" can be a hard one to make.

As we saw earlier, Match.com allows you to send winks without being a subscriber, but you can't reply to winks or exchange e-mails unless you subscribe. Also you cannot see a member's whole profile without subscribing. E-mails are protected by the "double-blind" system pioneered by Match.com. And it is one of the sites beginning to offer its members the use of mobile phones and text messaging, currently available as a subscription service in the US.

YAHOO! PERSONALS: USER-FRIENDLY AND GENEROUS IN FEATURES

Yahoo! Personals is of course part of the massive Yahoo! portal, currently with in excess of four hundred million users. Its dating arm, Yahoo! Personals, is in the top ten in Canada and the UK and is among the top three in the US.

Yahoo! Personals combines extreme user-friendliness with a cheerful generosity of features. Its extensive member profile includes thirty-two different parameters (including TV watching habits), and when you do a search, all those parameters are laid out in a vertical column on the left of your screen, so you can see exactly what you asked for and you can make adjustments on the go. When you press on any parameter it opens up and you see the choices available to you. Not only that, but you can specify for each feature whether it is a "must have" or not, and the search will be weighted accordingly. There is a keyword search.

Yahoo! recommends what personality type your mate should have, but if you feel feisty you can also just overrule their opinion, and issue your own verdict on which of Yahoo's twelve personality types your mate should be.

We will see in a moment that a relatively new breed of more expensive sites offers to do the matchmaking for you, with the help of a personality test. Yahoo! Personals does provide this sort of service in a separate department called Premier, but it also good-naturedly allows its ordinary subscribers to get in on the Personality game without spending an extra dime, by taking its free ten-minute "Personality and Love Style" test and factoring the results into their matching. Unlike many sites based on personality testing, Yahoo! Personals allows you to take the test *over again* if you want, and to offer feedback on its results so that they can *improve the test*. Yahoo! recommends what personality type your mate should have, but if you feel feisty you can also just overrule their opinion, and issue your own verdict on which of Yahoo's twelve personality types your mate should be. Is he an explorer, a leader, a rebel, a creator, or one of the other eight types? His love style can be one of six, which include the commendable "Careful" as well as the more obvious "Spontaneous" and "Romantic," and again you can make that choice if you want to, or make no choice. This democratic approach to personality types is very different from the "top-down" model of eHarmony, which we'll look at in a moment.

When you see someone you are interested in on Yahoo! Personals, you can send him an "Ice-breaker" (wink) even if you are not a subscriber, and you can reply to one "Ice-break-er." Once you subscribe, you can send and receive e-mails and Instant Messages. You can also record a video greeting or a voice greeting, for people to enjoy when they view your profile.

LAVALIFE.COM: FLEXIBLE, CUTTING-EDGE, AND EASY ON THE CREDIT CARD

Launched in Toronto in 2001 as a re-brand of webpersonals. com, Lavalife is one of Canada's leading dating sites, with over seven million members and over 600,000 paying members. In January 2005, Lavalife partnered with Sympatico.MSN.ca, Canada's leading Web portal. It is also aggressively expanding in the US and Australia.

This stylish site offers three separate environments: Dating, Relationship, and Intimate. (Most of its users are in the first two.)

I already mentioned Lavalife's unique payment strategy: You buy credits and pay as you go; there is no automatic re-newing or recharging. Credits cost $15 for 50, $25 for 100, $40 for 200. Six credits will buy you a 20-minute Instant Messaging session, or a first e-mail to a given member. The good news is that once you've e-mailed a certain member once, *all subsequent e-mails to that person are free.* That means that for a $15 out-lay you can e-mail eight members forever. Further favourable twists: All replies to e-mails and IMs are free. You can also send an e-mail "collect" and have the recipient decide whether to spring for it.

Lavalife's search page is notable for its copious supply of *one-click* options. To give four examples, with a single click you can go to local men within five years of your age, men online now with a picture, local men who are new to the site, or any search you have saved in the past. Search results are laid out in an unusual way, with a concise layout of Personal Details next to the photo and headline. That way you can glean quite a bit of information on first look (including religion, body type, smoking and drinking habits, children, education, and income). You can also jump directly to the member's video greeting, if he recorded one, and hear and see him in living colour. This is a feature whose value has to be experienced to be appreciated. When you open a profile you get the member's Introduction ("In My Own Words"), interests, and a section that lists what he wants to Have In Common.

And here is where Lavalife gets even more interesting. If a member has posted additional photos or videos, these are sequestered in an area called their "Backstage," to which *they* control access. That means you don't share your whole photo set with just anyone who visits the site. If a member is inter-ested enough in you to want to visit your Backstage, *they* have to request your permission; you can then take a look at their profile and photo and decide whether to give them access.

Lavalife also has a highly developed mobile service, which allows members to "click" with each other via cell phones that are equipped with text messaging or WAP browsing. In

Canada, Lavalife Mobile costs fifty cents for every message you send; there is no cost for messages you receive. (The charges appear on your wireless phone bill.)

All of these sites are great places to begin your advanced search for Mr. Right—check them out along with any others that appeal to you. I will conclude this tour of top dating sites by looking at heavy-duty matchmaking sites such as eHarmony, in the next chapter.

27

MATCHMAKING SITES

The Curious Case of
eHarmoney.com

$\mathcal{M}$ost good dating sites offer matching based on the characteristics you specify in your profile. These matches are also used as bait to get you more involved in the site: Unless you say no, they will send you e-mails showing you photos of your new matches, and will have them ready for you when you log onto the site. This can be a useful way of tracking new arrivals on the site, or ads you've overlooked.

In recent times one site has taken matchmaking beyond all others, at least in terms of visibility. That is eHarmony.com, launched in 2000 by psychologist Dr. Neil Clark Warren. Warren and his team claim to have figured out how to match people with each other, by using "deeper" criteria than the others— twenty-nine dimensions in all. eHarmony encourages you to hand over the heavy lifting to them. Go through their marathon personality test, and then sit back while they do the rest.

Consider the image they project on their powerful TV ads (which have an $80 million annual budget). A wise, older man smiles at you from the screen and conveys a message that might be expressed as follows [my words, not his]: *Don't worry about finding Mr. Right, I'll do it for you. I am the guru of true love. Look at these romping couples who have found happiness when I paired them off. I will read your soul and then find the person whose soul matches yours.*

That jolly white-haired figure on the TV screen looks to me a lot like our old friend, Destiny.

If any of this strikes an intriguing chord from our first chapter, it should. That jolly white-haired figure on the TV screen looks to me a lot like our old friend, Destiny. It's as though he's enticing you to give up the responsibility of selecting your own mate, and surrender to his romantic "magic." That way you can have the experience of feeling that it was meant to be, written in the stars. If you submit your needs to an inscrutable agency that understands you better than you do yourself, that agency will find your true love.

What a relief to let slip the reins of your romantic life! Just when you thought you had to tackle the problem using your own brain and your own skills—you don't!

PERSONALITY TESTS

In normal life (including normal online life) we notice a person, get interested, and then by interacting with them we find out whether there's a fit; and that is the approach I developed in Part Two. eHarmony proposes to by-pass this time-honoured process with an amazing short cut. They will tell you in advance—before you have even set eyes on the other person—whether the two of you will be able to get along in the long-term. They will weed through their massive membership (over ten million) and find your soulmate. How do they do this? With a personality test, and a theory about which personalities go well together in marriage. Those are the main things you are paying for when you subscribe.

When you use their service, you are making a double bet:

- That they will get your personality "right" (if such a concept is meaningful);
- That they have really figured out which male personalities are compatible with which female personalities.

Modern personality tests began in the early twentieth century as attempts to detect abnormal psychology, then evolved over the years into an instrument that claims to pigeonhole normal people too.

There are many problems with personality tests, but perhaps the biggest one is this: There is no way to test the tests. There is no objective scientific standard for measuring human "personality" (by which the scientists really seem to mean character), so there is nothing to measure the tests against. Therefore in a sort of bootstrap way, the tests have become their own justification.

If you look at the history of personality tests, you'll find that it's a series of fads that come and go. Rorschach's inkblot test (1921) conquers the world and then goes out of favour, succeeded by a long line of others, such as the Minnesota Multiphasic Personality Inventory (MMPI), Myers-Briggs, and the Five-Factor Model. Each test takes on an intimidating authority while it's in favour, then is increasingly met with scepticism.

The second great problem with personality tests is that they are superficial. They ask general questions with no context. They can't get down to details, there isn't time. If their philosophy were put in a nutshell, it would be: *by asking shallow, vague questions we hope to get deep, precise results.*

In addition, personality tests are at times confusing and ambiguous, and at other times simple to see through. They make honesty way more difficult than it should be, *and* they are easy to fool.

Then there is the "Furor" effect, worth watching out for. Also known as the "personal validation fallacy," it states that almost any description, if suitably nuanced with contrasts, can seem true of you. ("You are very social, yet you treasure your alone time.") The Furor effect has kept countless astrologers employed for centuries.

Robert Frost said, "Poetry is what gets lost in translation." When you try to translate poetry into another language, you may be able to hang on to the basic meaning, but you'll lose one thing: the *poetic* quality. Frost might equally have said that *personality is what gets lost in testing.*

eHARMONY PROCESS

After you take its 436-question test, eHarmony comes back with a Personality profile and a Compatibility profile. They then start finding matches for you. Matches are shown in summary form, with topics such as interests, life skills, and relationship strengths, some answered in the member's own words. Photos are not shown until you subscribe, and even then many members choose not to share photos until a later stage.

eHarmony costs $59.95 for one month, less if you commit to more months, with the cheapest plan being $251.40 for a year.

Subscribers can pursue a match, by being taken through stages of "Guided Communication," in which the two of you exchange five questions and answers from boilerplate lists provided by the site, then exchange ten "must haves" and "can't stands," then ask three more questions which you can write yourself if you want. If all goes well you then move to the "Open Communication" stage, which can be reached earlier if both parties elect to "FastTrack."

In the Open Communication stage you can exchange e-mails with your match and move towards meeting.

Frost might equally have said that personality is what gets lost in testing. Let's look at some pros and cons of eHarmony. (Some of these points apply equally to other matchmaking sites such as Chemistry.com, PerfectMatch.com, and Yahoo! Personals Premier.)

CONS OF eHARMONY

1. eHarmony won't let you browse its members. This is par for the course on matchmaking sites but it's still worth pondering. They have millions of sincere, paying clients on their roster, but you can't explore them for yourself, and they can't look at you. *You are only allowed to see the people whom eHarmony says you can see.*

2. In an eHarmony TV ad, Dr. Neil Clark Warren chuckles and says, "Experience what it feels like when attraction is ignited by deep compatibility." That makes it sound as if they find people you're attracted to, then narrow that down by choosing the ones you are deeply compatible with. But it doesn't work that way. They find lots of "matches" for you, you gradually get to know some of them if there is mutual interest, and somewhere along the line you see a photo (or the actual person) and find out what that does to the equation.

It must be said on the plus side that if eHarmony has truly selected all your potential soulmates from its active membership, then at least you are heading for the right people's photos.

3. eHarmony's test can't be corrected. After you take their test, eHarmony issues you a lengthy Personality Profile. Now what happens if you take one look at this and can tell that it is wrong? Suppose you know yourself pretty well and you can just see that they have described someone very different from you. You show the profile to three of your best friends and they all agree that it is laughably off-target. (It says that you are obedient, conservative, a follower, and not into impulsive plans. But in fact you are known to be adventurous, rebellious, and a natural leader.)

Can you take the test again, hoping for a more accurate result? No. Apparently, like the Pope, their test is infallible. (In fact they make you promise that you will only take the test once.)

Can you ask eHarmony to correct the profile? No. Which may make you wonder why your humble assistance in describing your own personality is not welcomed.

(And this is where a nutty idea often occurs to me about personality tests. A lot of their questions rely on the user's honesty and self-knowledge [the "trick" questions that supposedly expose dishonesty are notoriously unreliable and easy to scam]. So, Mr. Personality Tester, instead of making a mysterious leap from my assorted answers to your conclusions about me, why not give me your array of possible *conclusions* and let me assemble my own final profile?)

At any rate, if eHarmony described your personality wrongly, that leaves you in a strange situation. The more stringent their matching machine is (and they say it is very stringent), the *less* likely you are to be matched with anybody you'll be suited to. Not a happy situation

4. If you want to have fun with personality types, you can do it more cheaply on Yahoo! Personals, and be in control. You can take their free ten-minute Personality and Love Style test, and Yahoo! will give you reports (Your Personality Type, Your Love Style, and Your Biggest Challenge) and resulting matches. While reading the reports you are offered highlight points with which you can agree or disagree—the stated purpose being: "Please give us your feedback to help us improve this test." You can also opt to take the Yahoo! test again if you want. When searching you can choose what personality types if any you want to meet. (The odd thing is, once you're put in control you may find that you don't want to narrow people down in that way. You may stop and wonder about all the fabulous folks that eHarmony wouldn't let you see.)

PROS OF eHARMONY

1. If you believe in personality tests, and you believe that scientists can tell which personalities are matched, and you can afford their fees, eHarmony will do all the work for you and find you men who, for starters, have those beliefs in common with you. There are a lot of people online. If you are short on time, they will certainly narrow the field for you.

2. You can take the eHarmony personality test for free, and if you don't agree with its resulting portrait of you and your mate, don't pay the fee to join.

3. Photos often don't do justice to the person; you can be turned off by a bad photo, thinking the person isn't attractive,

when really the problem is that the photo failed to capture their attractiveness. eHarmony can lead you to someone, make you take an interest in him for other reasons; and perhaps get you past a bad photo. On the other hand you could accomplish the same thing by choosing not to look at the photos on any other dating site. (Ask yourself how likely you are to do that.)

4. You may be someone who isn't that affected by a person's appearance, and you may be looking for the same. eHarmony will help you downplay that dimension.

5. eHarmony has an eye-catching track record for bringing about marriages between its subscribers, as many as 16,630 within a twelve-month period.

6. Because of its higher price, its stated goals, and its track record, eHarmony tends to attract users who are really sincere about finding a long-term relationship.

7. Suppose you take the eHarmony test and then you receive your Personality Profile and your Compatibility Profile. After carefully reading both of these, you find that you strongly agree with their detailed portraits of you and the sort of person you would be good with. You then receive your first few matches, and although you can't see their photos, you love everything about them. With such encouragement that hasn't cost you anything, you may well have reason to take the plunge.

OTHER SITES

If you do decide to go the route of personality-based matchmaking, there are several sites besides eHarmony that are worth a look. Chemistry.com, an offshoot of Match.com, was launched in January 2006. Its personality test is based on four types: the

Explorer, the Builder, the Negotiator, and the Director. (Members are also assigned a secondary type.) An example of matching philosophy: Explorers are said to do well with Builders. When you open a profile you can see photos, without subscribing. Body type can be specified and is well handled as on Match. com. Cost is $49.95 a month with the usual discounts for longer periods. Other interesting sites involving personality tests include Yahoo! Personals Premier (not to be confused with the free test described above), PerfectMatch.com, Tickle.com, and LoveHappens.com.

28

GETTING TO KNOW HIM

$\mathcal{L}$et's say you have done some prospecting on dating sites, found one you like, and subscribed to it. The real action begins now. You've started getting responses to your ad, or you have responded to some ads and some of those men have returned your interest. So you look through their e-mails, you check their profiles, you look at photos and words, and you get impressions.

And a few of them strike you as possibilities. If you're a rookie, something in you may still feel sceptical even of these, but they are interested in you and you can't just ignore this fact.

So you e-mail them back, and one thing leads to another, and soon your list is narrowing.

As it narrows, you are eliminating a bunch of Mr. Wrongs. Here are some important tips about that.

POINTERS ABOUT MESSRS. WRONG

1. Men Who Don't Appeal to You
Don't waste a lot of time responding to men who don't strike

your fancy. Unless they are over the top, they will probably not think twice if they don't hear back from you. If you do try to explain why you aren't interested, you will only arouse their interest more, or maybe their need to argue.

2. Men Who Are Too Lovesick from the Get-Go

If a man *does* come on really strong based on your ad alone, or even based on your having e-mailed him before there's been any real dialogue between you, watch out. A man who gets too enamoured too fast—when he hasn't met you or even heard your voice—is probably a needy soul living in a fantasy world. If you feel you must respond, tell him you've found someone and are no longer looking. Then delete all replies you get from him, or on sites that offer the feature, block him. In other words, ignore him. He'll go away.

Why do I say this? Well, look at it this way. If a man is willing to go nuts over you even though you've had no real dialogue and he's never spoken to you and you haven't met, he is probably projecting his dearest fantasy on you. It may have been triggered by your photo, which he finds irresistible, or it could be something in your profile (less likely), but he is so desperate to fill his order at the supermarket of love that he can't be bothered with niceties like knowing you at all.

A man like this is so desperate to fill his order at the supermarket of love that he can't be bothered with niceties like knowing you at all.

I'm not saying a man shouldn't go crazy over your ad, shouldn't gaze at your photo and forget to eat or drink. All I'm saying is that the *right* guy, the one you're looking for, knows how to play it cool, at least cool enough not to invade your emotional space with big demands before you've even met. If a man seems very excited about encountering you but does a decent job of keeping it under control, if he flirts without crowding you or smothering you, he may well be the one you want.

3. Men Who Obviously Just Want Sex, and Are Too Dumb to Hide That Fact

Ignore them. Block them. Don't reply. They'll go away.

4. Men Who Don't Live in Your Area

I'm taking a deep breath: this is a thorny one. Let's suppose you made a rule for yourself that you only wanted to deal with men who live within a reasonable radius of you, say fifty miles. So you were careful not to contact any men who were farther away. You may have gazed at a few wonderful ads of men in distant cities, and some of them may have made you sigh, but you stuck to your guns and didn't reach out to them.

But now someone has contacted you, in response to your ad. And he sounds like the best of the bunch so far, and he looks great, and he lives two thousand miles away. What do you do?

It all depends. The main reason *not* to pursue it is so important that I will make it an axiom.

Once you find someone you know you are really interested in, the sooner you meet him in person the better.

I will go into this in more detail in a moment; for now just take it on faith, you don't want to spend weeks or months cultivating a bond with someone without meeting in person. So the long-distance dude is a problem. Unless you travel a lot and can get to him, or vice versa, you are shopping for trouble. And there's this little hitch: What if you do meet and you really fall for each other and then you're stuck in a long-distance relationship?

- Is one of you ready and willing to move to the other's city?
- Even if your/his employment situation would allow that, are you/he capable of taking that emotional risk for anyone?

I'm not saying the answer to these questions has to be no. I *can't* say that, because in fact I met my Ms. Right online and she lived 800 miles away and eventually one of us moved; but I do have to say that things would have been a lot easier if we had started out in the same town. And I also have to say that long-distance relationships are generally a pain, and generally don't have happy endings.

So unless you can answer yes to my two questions, and unless you are totally knocked out by each other, it is far better to avoid the temptation of the distant online lover.[1] And the best way to do that is, *don't search outside your area.*

5. Men Who Aren't Compatible with You

As you search for men who might interest you, and as you exchange e-mails with the lucky ones who do, it is the perfect time to apply the lessons of Part Two. Recall the parameters of compatibility that I covered, and recall the thoughts you had about yourself and the man you are looking for as you read them. As you look at a man's ad and e-mails, keep in mind parameters such as life goals, sense of humour, body issues, culture, politics, and religion. Don't hesitate to explore these areas when they arise, and watch out for red flags and deal-breakers.

---

1. There is one plus side to long-distance relationships worth mentioning. Because you don't have the distraction of each other's physical presence, you tend to get to know each other very thoroughly. You learn how to talk and listen to each other, and you learn huge amounts about each other's past and present lives. In other words, the friendship tends to be developed, and tested, very thoroughly.

When you're actually talking to someone online or by phone, all of the compatibility parameters are fair game, and you can often learn enough to screen someone out. In a sense you'll be acting as your own matchmaker, and the more you do this, the more you may realize it's not a task you want to entrust to anyone else.

One last pointer before I go on.

GIVING OUT YOUR LOCATOR INFORMATION

Don't be overly generous with information that could lead someone to your door, until you have a solid sense of him. There used to be a spy-v.-spy atmosphere online, and people would use aliases and do anything to conceal their basic information. Now things have relaxed a little as the Internet has become part of our natural environment, but there are still cautions to be observed.

When you're getting to know an appealing guy, you are going to tell him a lot of stuff—how can you not? He already has your photo, and knows what metropolitan area you live in. He probably knows your first name, because it's hard to be friendly in e-mails without giving this. Some people prefer to use a false name until they feel very sure of the other person, and there's nothing wrong with that. Do it if it makes you feel more comfortable.

Until you feel sure that someone is okay, don't give your last name. Don't make your last name part of your handle on the dating site (or on your own e-mail that you use with people you don't trust yet)! Talk about the type of work you do, but don't narrow it down so far that the guy can figure out what building you work in. Don't rave about the wonderful view from your apartment to the point where the guy can deduce your address. This kind of *locator* information is too precious to give out casually.

What do I mean by feeling sure of someone? Most people online are sane, hard-working, well-meaning specimens, but a few might overreact to the charms of you, or to the zest of your early e-mails. There is no hard and fast rule about how well you have to know someone before you can get free with your info. It's like in real life: You have to trust your instincts. I'm sure you've had the experience of meeting someone at a bar or a party and you hit it off so quickly that you told war stories about your employers and you met the next day for lunch (he picked you up at your job). If you have lots of experience with meeting people online, you can probably sometimes tell right away that a guy is okay. If you are less experienced, a good rule of thumb is this: Don't give out your locator info until you have at least talked to the person on the phone (without giving him your number).

There may come a point, fairly early on, when you and he want to e-mail each other directly, not through the anonymous service of the Web site where you met. By all means accept his direct e-mail and give him yours, unless you feel that your e-mail address contains too much information at the point you've reached (e.g. it might reveal your employer or your last name). If you have an anonymous e-mail address, use that at first. (These can easily be created for free at such Web portals as Hotmail and Yahoo!)

Other than that, how should you conduct yourself as you get to know men online?

Be yourself, have fun, trust your instincts, don't give in to euphoria too easily, and above all, try not to fall in love.

That's right. Don't fall in love with someone you haven't met in person. I will devote part of the next chapter to this pitfall.

Trust your instincts, but remember this. People are a lot better at sizing each other up in person than they are online. You may get a good read on his intellect, or his interests, or his writing ability, but you don't know him until you see him with your own eyes. Sightings don't occur online. They may *seem* to occur, but you can't get a thorough sense of someone from a couple of photos and some words on a screen, not the way you can when you are standing face to face. And even sightings often turn out to be wrong; they have to be tested by experience. Real-world experience. In person.

The only thing that can stop our amazing ability to project fantasies onto people is being with them in person. And even that sometimes doesn't stop us!

You can easily find out enough online to know you need to meet that guy. But not enough to fall in love. Even when you talk on the phone and it's fantastic, it's not enough.

Which leads us to my next topic.

THE FIRST PHONE CALL

After you've spilled your dreams and sorrows to each other in e-mails, after a holy host of LOLs, you want to hear each other's voices live. (On some sites you may have already seen and heard each other's video greetings or IMs.) That's natural, and good. So you tell him you'd like to call him.

You don't have him call you. That would involve *locator* information. And life ain't fair. Dudes have to give up their phone numbers, women don't.

If he has any problem with you calling him, walk away. End it. The most likely reason he doesn't want you to call is that he's attached, married, taken. Lots of married men are out there trolling for women. Some of them just want to have a fantasy affair; some may be searching for their next relationship; some want an affair now and are hoping to deceive the one they're with and you. You don't need any of them.

Ideally your unattached prospect will want you to call him at home on a land line. Second best is at home on a cell phone. Third best is at work, mostly because it's hard to talk at work. When you do call him, by all means block your phone number from appearing on his caller ID, by using *67 or whatever other means you have.

What I hope will happen is that you already have an excellent rapport that the two of you developed in e-mails, and then you call him and find it's even better on the phone, you get on famously, and you can't wait to meet each other. So you do.

But it doesn't always go that well on that telephone line. Sometimes the charming, articulate person who lit up your screen, disappears.

How could this happen? Well, maybe he is very shy. Maybe he is a talented writer who is really good at weaving a spell when he's at a keyboard—and maybe this spell is formed out of his own deepest thoughts, but he's too awkward to express them in a social context. Or maybe he is clamming up because it's threatening to get real.

Or your Romeo could disappear because you don't like the way he talks. You may not like his voice, or his accent, or his vocabulary. Or his personality. Once you're on the phone you'll be able to tell new things about him, important things.

Does he listen? Does he ask good questions? Is he funny? Is he slick? Is he full of himself? Is he genuinely interested in you?

Is he boring?

New facts will come to light, very quickly, and he'll be getting the very same take on you. On the phone people are likely to be less guarded, less composed than they were online. A joke, a word, can suddenly reveal things that were carefully hidden before.

When Meg Called Dennis

Meg had been talking to Dennis online for two weeks when she first called him. He seemed like a nice guy, they'd been joking around a lot, he was burly and handsome in his photo. Meg had specified in her ad that she didn't want anything to do with the isms: racism, sexism, ageism. And Dennis had never said anything online that threw up a red flag. But on the phone, something bothered her. He seemed cruder. A short way into the conversation, he referred to someone he worked with as a "bitch." Meg didn't mind that he didn't like the woman, but she minded the way he used the word "bitch."

"I could tell he thought that women had special faults that men are never guilty of," she says.

She let that pass. Then Dennis started talking about football. He was laughing to himself about how his Jets had mashed Miami, arguing with himself about the fine points of Monday's game, just going on and on. Meg liked some sports, but what really ticked her off during this first phone call was that Dennis didn't check in with her to gauge her interest level. "He just *assumed* I was fascinated," she says. "That I knew all the teams and cared about them. I guess he didn't bother to ask me, because he thinks women have to say they love football to please their men. I finally got him off the phone and never talked to him after that."

After you've spilled your dreams and sorrows to each other in e-mails, after a holy host of LOLs, you want to hear each other's voices live.

More often, though, the first phone call is like a window opening on a very nice view. For the first time you can directly perceive the person who used to be only words on a screen. It's the thrill of the real. You hear his voice and suddenly he is an individual. That voice has a particular timbre and it's wonderful listening to it. It's the first sensory contact the two of you, who reached out to each other in cyberspace, have had. Now you can *hear* how each other's minds work. It's easier to talk, the humour is sharper. Even the pauses, the quiet moments, tell you something. So the two of you take the next step towards the real world.

More phone calls follow, and the subject of meeting comes up.

The more promising he is, the sooner you should meet.

As soon as you have talked with him on the phone and you are sure you are interested in him, propose a meeting. Why do I say this? Well, it's because the worst thing you can do is get way ahead of yourselves emotionally, before you've even met. We'll talk about the first meeting, and why it should be earlier rather than later, in the next chapter.

29

THE FIRST IN-PERSON MEETING

Fearlessly Facing the Possibilities (One of Which is Very Good)

$\mathscr{I}$t's a little odd when you first meet someone you've only known online. The two of you have a history together, yet you've never seen each other. So that history hangs by a thread: It can crash to the ground in a moment. It can suddenly turn into a false history, even though it seemed so real.

So it's a nervous moment as you walk into that café. But if the two of you have kept your expectations in check, if you've agreed to meet early on, before you got ahead of yourselves, the nervousness isn't so bad. The worst that can happen is that you have a coffee with a nice person and nothing comes of it. Or you make a friend.

And the best that can happen is that the two of you take an immediate shine to each other. Even then there's an adjustment. No guy is going to look exactly as you had pictured him—you won't either. You two will be thrown back to where nature has you, the *starting line*. On nature's scorecard, nothing counts that happened before. The meter wasn't running yet. This is the first time you've directly seen, heard, touched, and smelled each other, and nature is working overtime to assimilate all the incoming data. You will probably be shy, you may be awkward and giggly. That's all fine, you can deal with it, it's good fun.

In fact, when you find the right person it's more than good fun: It's a delight. For the first time you get the texture of someone. That's way better than a photo. You see the crinkles next to their eyes, the texture of their hair, their bone structure, their smile, their hands.

WHY IT'S BETTER TO MEET EARLY IN THE PROCESS

I said in the last chapter that you should propose a meeting as soon as you are definitely interested in someone. That is for the following reason. If the two of you have let yourselves get too amorous, too romantic, if you've let yourselves dream that you're in love *and then you don't hit it off*, the crash can be a noisy one. You walk into the café, you look around, and you pray that the one at the corner table isn't him. But it is. And you know right away he isn't your type. But you've been making love to him online. It's awkward, it's embarrassing.

On nature's scorecard, nothing counts that happened before.

Or he rises to greet you and he looks even better than his photos, but his handshake seems lifeless; and when you sit down he doesn't act like the warm, engaging, even adoring guy you thought he was. This can be because he is somehow let down by you, and rather than bluntly tell you such an unkind thing, he is trying to spare your feelings by driving you away.

But enough of these "too much too soon" scenarios: They're easily avoided. And awkward as they are, they aren't life-threatening. Just remember that a major pitfall of online romance is *falling in love before you meet in person*. And the best way to avoid that pitfall is to meet early, as soon as you know you're truly interested in someone.

Let's get back to that first meeting. Where should it be? A café is good, a quiet bar—a safe place, a public place, indoors, a place where it's easy to talk. Set aside half an hour. Don't commit in advance to dinner, or to some outing that will take all afternoon. Those things can wait till the second meeting, or if you really hit it off, you can always change plans on the spur of the moment. If you *don't* hit it off you'll want to exit quickly and gracefully, not be moored together for a three-course meal.

What should you wear? I'm not an expert on women's garb, but from my simple male point of view I would tell you this: Be tasteful but sexy. Let him see you. Don't obscure your good points. Don't let fear cramp your style. Don't be afraid he won't like you and decide not to wear your knockout blouse. If he doesn't like you, he isn't the right guy. Imagine that you are playing a part in a movie called, "The woman who went to a café and met the man who would later fall in love with her." Wear what that character would wear.

HOW TO AVOID THE FEAR OF FAILURE

So you're sitting across from him and things are going pretty well. What do you say? What do you watch for and watch out for? What should your agenda be?

The short answer is, it's better not to have an agenda. You may be wanting magic. But it's hard to have an epiphany when you've planned and hoped for exactly that. Life's best moments usually come unbidden. Like cats, they don't jump onto your lap when you want them to. So the best thing you can do is relax and be entertained, take it as it comes, and like a Zen master, *don't be attached to a certain outcome.* You're going to meet lots of men this way, and lots of them won't be the right guy. So this particular guy doesn't need to be.

Not expecting a certain outcome brings several advantages with it. One is, you are not so distracted by what you want to happen, that you can't see what *is* happening. You stay cool, aware of what's really going on, how you're reacting, how he's reacting, what he's like.

The second advantage of not writing the script in advance is that you don't have to be anxious about failure. You don't walk in thinking, "Oh god, what if he doesn't like me?" You don't worry that you won't do well enough, that you won't live up to your (or his) script. You keep in mind that if it's a test at all, it's not you that is being tested, it's a potential couple. You're there to see how the *couple* does.

Just be natural and go where your conversational impulses take you. If the meeting doesn't flow fairly easily, you're probably with the wrong guy. When in doubt, ask him about himself. Notice whether he asks you about you. Notice whether he listens, whether he asks follow-up questions or is always just waiting to make his next point.

About now you may be expecting me to say something like this: Bring to the café a clipboard on which you've put a list of "Kearns' Fifteen Factors for Compatibility," and ask clever questions in all those areas, scoring the candidate's replies in the right-hand column. Not so much. My study of compatibility in Part Two of this book was meant to stimulate your thoughts, spark your own intuitions, and make your antennae alert, so that you are more likely to recognize the clues that mean "kindred spirit" to you, and to notice the warning signs of a man who isn't right for you. Most of this isn't going to happen on day one, however.

What will happen is that some preliminary questions get answered—maybe.

There are two main questions.

- Do you get along as people—do you find it pleasant to spend time together?
- Do you find each other physically attractive? (= romantically, sexually)

If you don't get along as people, chances are it ain't goin' anywhere, better to bag it.

So let's assume the talk flows easily and you find each other likable. Then there are four basic outcomes on the romantic front:

THE FOUR OUTCOMES

One. You both are attracted and want to meet again. Smiles all around.

Two. You both aren't interested. This is not such a bad outcome, because you will probably be at ease with each other, may have an entertaining time, and if you like each other enough as people, you may have found a new friend.

Three. He is attracted but you aren't. Bad news, but it doesn't hurt your ego.

Four. You are attracted but he isn't. This may be the hardest to detect, if you are distracted by your reaction to him or if he is less than candid. If you find that your own body language is way more forward than his, you may be in outcome Four. Lay back a bit and see what he does. If it becomes obvious that he isn't interested, so be it. Mr. Right, you will remember, most definitely is interested, so be polite, end the date sooner rather than later, and then go check your e-mail.

WHAT HAPPENS NEXT

There will come a day when you find yourself in outcome One. You get along as people, you are both attracted to each other, and you wear out your smile muscles in the first hour. You agree to meet again, and you go home on cloud nine.

Don't be afraid he won't like you and decide not to wear your knockout blouse.

At that point, it ceases to matter that you met on the Internet. The two of you have made it to the real world, you're on solid ground now, and your journey of discovery has begun. You may know more about each other than most people do after one date, but what you still have to learn is much more important. Still, you both deserve congratulations, because you went out into the cyber universe and found a good one. Now you can start accumulating real experiences together.

How this goes will determine whether this man is the lifetime partner you're looking for, or not. Keeping in mind the ground I covered in Part Two of this book, you won't be inclined to make snap judgments. You won't condemn him for having baggage: You'll look for how he *handles* his baggage. You won't let sexual attraction blind you to the other facets of your relationship. You'll appreciate that his ability to admit his imperfections is a good thing, not a bad thing. As you get to know him, you'll be aware of how his attitudes fit with yours, regarding talking/sharing, body issues, TV, religion, children, and so many others. You'll pay attention to humour, how it unfolds between the two of you—knowing that it goes to the heart of the matter. You won't mind if everything isn't a perfect fit: You aren't looking for a clone of yourself. But you'll be glad if the rich areas you do have in common outweigh the little frictions. (Because you met online, you have the advantage of already having screened out many men whose basic stances would have been a problem.)

When it does start to seem as if you may have found the soulmate you were looking for, take a deep breath. As Sinatra once said, take it nice and easy. Over the weeks and months, enjoy the process of finding a place in each other's lives. Enjoy the fact that you are happier and less stressed than you used to be.

And maybe one day you'll be having lunch together and you'll be talking in your animated way and suddenly he'll reach out and take your hand, and you won't remember what you were just saying, but you'll know that whatever it was, it must have struck him as pretty amazing, because he is looking at you like you've never been looked at before.

ACKNOWLEDGEMENTS

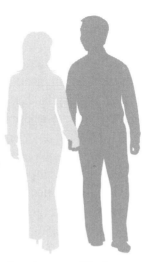

$\mathcal{T}$he journey of a first book to publication is an unlikely passage from "fanciful long shot" to "meant to be," but the author always remembers how things looked back at the start. That the journey was completed is due to the timely help of a number of people, and I am glad of this occasion to thank them.

I want to thank esteemed writer Marni Jackson for looking at my manuscript at an early stage, when it was easier to see what needed fixing than what had merit. She nevertheless saw value in it, and she rolled up her sleeves and showed me in what direction it needed to move. Not content with that, she then furnished the happy idea of a submission to Ian Brown for his collection of men's writings, *What I Meant To Say*. That set in motion a train of events for which I am deeply grateful.

For their support and encouragement I want to thank Ian Brown, whose excellent collection honoured my work by association; Janice Zawerbny, first editor of my chapter "How Men Choose Women;" Sheree-Lee Olson, Style Editor at *The Globe and Mail*, who gave me an outlet for Valentine musings; and Georgie Binks, early reviewer and fellow writer, whose enthusiasm and thoughtfulness connected me to my excellent agent.

Working with that agent, Sam Hiyate of The Rights Factory, has been a romp and an inspiration from the start, and I thank him for his unquenchable fire. Sam has kept me in the loop and has worked me hard as a hands-on participant in the promotional process. He is always a voice of optimism and reason.

I want to thank my publisher Jennifer Smith and her team at John Wiley & Sons Canada, Ltd. who have treated me better than an author should expect at every step of the way, and have allowed me more input into their process than was truly prudent.

For her honesty, kindness, and wonderfully astute brain, I thank my editor, Leah Marie Fairbank. Without ever speaking a discouraging word she managed to alert me to problems subtle and blatant, almost making me believe that needed rewrites were my idea. She also dispensed enough praise to keep the wind in my sails, and tossed in enough charm and humour to make the task of revision seem like a lark.

I thank Julia Kellaway and her team at Vermilion in London for embracing a book from across the Atlantic and providing an exciting design with a fresh perspective.

A number of other people read the manuscript at various stages and gave valuable feedback; for this I thank Julie McElroy, Gordon Vincent, Nancy Granick, Natalie Sciscio, Kathy Cressman, and Rachel Owen. My research for the book involved give-and-take with countless men and women whom I thank for their forthrightness and insights. I also thank Vanderbilt University Library for the use of its excellent research resources.

Finally, I want to thank my partner, Debra Donahue, for the many gifts her presence bestows on me. A connoisseur of male–female psychology, she has educated me in more ways than I can name, and has regaled me with many fine stories that were grist for my mill. She has also lent stability and warmth to a life that sorely needed those things, and has risked her sanity and her heart in order to join me on this writer's ride.